100 Ideas for Secondary Teachers:

Outstanding MFL Lessons

Dannielle Warren

BLOOMSBURY EDUCATION

LONDON   OXFORD   NEW YORK   NEW DELHI   SYDNEY

BLOOMSBURY EDUCATION
Bloomsbury Publishing Plc
50 Bedford Square, London, WC1B 3DP, UK

BLOOMSBURY, BLOOMSBURY EDUCATION and the Diana logo are
trademarks of Bloomsbury Publishing Plc

First published in Great Britain, 2019 by Bloomsbury Publishing Plc

A catalogue record for this book is available from the British Library

ISBN: PB: 978-1-4729-6793-0; ePDF: 978-1-4729-6794-7;
ePub: 978-1-4729-6792-3

4 6 8 10 9 7 5

Typeset by Newgen KnowledgeWorks Pvt. Ltd., Chennai, India
Printed and bound by CPI Group (UK) Ltd, Croydon CR0 4YY

To find out more about our authors and books visit
www.bloomsbury.com and sign up for our newsletters

To George
May you never doubt your ability to achieve great things.

Contents

Acknowledgements

I somehow managed to write this book during my first year of motherhood, but I wouldn't have completed it without the help and support of the following people:

Thank you to my editors, Hannah Marston and Chloe Fitzsimmons, and to anyone else at Bloomsbury who has worked on this book, for helping to turn my childhood dream of writing a book into reality. It takes a village.

Thank you to Joe Dale, who launched the #mfltwitterati and created a platform for language teachers across the world to connect easily. Without him, I may not have been offered the opportunity to write this book.

Thank you to all the wise owls who share their fantastic teaching ideas online and via social media.

Thank you to all those colleagues who have supported me, especially Vera for double-checking my Spanish.

Thank you to my Auntie Jacqueline for reading through my ideas and correcting my German.

Thank you to Michèle for checking through the book for me and for your words of encouragement when I was doubting myself.

Thank you to all the incredible people who have kindly allowed me to share their ideas in this book.

Kirsty Hibberd – Get in order
Michèle Lefebvre-Smith – Registration conversation
Kayleigh Meyrick – Speaking ladders, Live writes, Emoji mindmaps
Stuart Gorse – Trapdoor
Stephen Lockyer – Structure strips
Mo Ladak – Sharing successes
Jennifer Beattie – Chocolate bar infinitives
Laura Scott – Be a smartie
Dr Gianfranco Conti – Mosaic writing
Bronagh Dooris – Highlighter splat
Karen Knight – Thinking quilts
Becky Russell – Revision clocks

Thank you to my family and friends for being my cheerleaders and convincing me to agree to writing this book during my maternity leave.

Thank you in particular to my parents, Sue and Dennis, who have always encouraged me to work hard and for regularly reminding me that the world is my 'lobster'.

And last but not least, thank you to my incredibly supportive husband, Pete, who did way more than his fair share of housework and parenting, making it possible for me to write this book.

Introduction

Languages are so important. They open up doors and bring people closer together. As teachers of modern foreign languages (MFL), we are in such a privileged position to be able to share our knowledge with young people, broadening their horizons and helping them to become the future interpreters and translators, the future facilitators and negotiators.

This book contains practical ideas to help make your MFL lessons outstanding. I feel like I should start by confessing to you that I am not always outstanding. To be honest, I don't know anyone who is. I'm not sure an always-outstanding teacher even exists, at least not if you want a life outside of the four walls of your classroom. With goalposts regularly being moved and the recipe for an outstanding MFL lesson changing often, it can be difficult to know where to start to improve the quality of your lessons, particularly if you are new to the profession. However, some things will always remain the same and for me a successful lesson is simply one where students are engaged and progressing. As long as we keep this at the heart of what we do, then we can't really go far wrong. When selecting the 100 ideas for this book, I have therefore focused on those that capture students' interest, inspire them and help them to thrive.

When reading this book, it is important to remember that every student is different, and while something may work well with one class, or indeed one student, it may not be a success with another. You should respond to what your students need, adapting activities where necessary. As the class teacher, you know your students best. The delivery of these ideas is just as important – don't be afraid to show your passion for your subject, as this will be infectious. It also helps to strike a balance between the familiar and unfamiliar – making sure you have established routines and good classroom management, while also keeping learning fresh and engaging, with some new and exciting lesson ideas.

Through social media, I've had the opportunity to connect and exchange ideas and resources with MFL teachers from all over the world. It is a privilege to be asked by Bloomsbury to produce this book and be able to share some of these ideas with an even wider audience. Most of the ideas in this book I have personally trialled and developed with my own students throughout my seven years of teaching. As well as my own creations, there are ideas I have picked up over the years from inspirational teachers who have allowed me to observe them doing what they do best and from kind teachers who have shared their wisdom and creativity via social media.

With the ever-increasing demands on us as teachers, I know personally how hard it can be to juggle the workload and maintain a relatively healthy work–life balance. I have therefore endeavoured to include a range of activities that require little to no preparation beforehand, as well as not too much marking afterwards. Additionally, I have added a ton of ready-to-use or easily adaptable resources to the 100 Ideas website. Hopefully this will make your job a little easier and give you more time at the weekend to do whatever it is that makes you smile.

I would love to hear how you use these ideas in your own classroom, so do get in touch with me @morganmfl on Twitter using the #100ideas hashtag or via my Facebook page www.facebook.com/morganmfl.

How to use this book

This book includes quick, easy and practical ideas for you to dip in and out of to help you deliver truly outstanding MFL lessons.

Each idea includes:

- a catchy title, easy to refer to and share with your colleagues
- an interesting quote linked to the idea
- a summary of the idea in bold, making it easy to flick through the book and identify an idea you want to use at a glance
- a step-by-step guide to implementing the idea.

Each idea also includes one or more of the following:

Teaching tip

Practical tips and advice for how and how not to run the activity or put the idea into practice.

Taking it further

Ideas and advice for how to extend the idea or develop it further.

Bonus idea ★

There are 35 bonus ideas in this book that are extra-exciting, extra-original and extra-interesting.

Share how you use these ideas and find out what other practitioners have done using **#100ideas**.

Online resources also accompany this book. When a resource is referenced in the book, follow the link www.bloomsbury.com/100-ideas-secondary-MFL to find extra resources, catalogued under the relevant idea number. Here you can also find the full list of website addresses mentioned in the book.

Speaking

Part 1

Dice discussions

'A fun way to get them speaking.'

This lovely, low-prep speaking activity also doubles up as a revision exercise that can be used in the run-up to a speaking exam.

Students can work in pairs or groups for this activity, with each group requiring a dice and a list of six topics chosen by you.

Allow the groups a few minutes to discuss the vocabulary – including questions and key phrases – that is needed for each of the chosen topics. They could brainstorm this on whiteboards, A3 paper or even on their desks if you have whiteboard pens that can be easily erased later. You then invite students to wander around the classroom and 'steal' some vocabulary from the other groups. When they have returned to their tables, students roll the dice and talk in their groups for as long as possible on the corresponding topic. They can use their brainstorms to help them, but may find they don't need to after a while. When they have finished discussing one topic, they can roll the dice again.

Don't worry if they roll the same number twice. The more they practise speaking about a topic, the better and quicker they will become at thinking on the spot and speaking spontaneously. At the end of the exercise, ask each group to discuss one topic in front of the class and reflect on what went well and how they would improve next time.

As with any speaking activity, it's important to establish some ground rules and make it clear that students should only be talking in the target language. Rewards could be given to encourage students to stay on-task, e.g. for the team who speak for the longest time.

Get in order

'A way to encourage pupil talk.'

This idea was inspired by Kirsty Hibberd, who teaches drama at Hounsdown School. Kirsty would sometimes use this Kagan Structure as a warm-up activity for the staff on INSET days, but it works really well as a quick starter activity in language lessons too!

Students are given a question that they have to ask each other and find out the answers to before lining up in a particular order – for example, 'When is your birthday?'. The challenge? Of course, they can only speak in the target language! Give students the task and ask them to come up with the question in the target language. They could first practise in pairs before circulating the classroom.

It would be useful to use a question that links to the previous lesson or which sets the context for today's lesson. For example:

- When is your birthday? (Students line up in age order.)
- Where did you last go on holiday? / Where do you live? (Students line up according to distance away from location of school.)
- How long do you spend watching television per day/week?
- How long do you spend playing video games per day/week?
- How long do you spend on your phone/ social media per day/week?
- How long do you spend reading books per day/week?

I've found that doing this regularly instils confidence in my students and it's another way of getting them asking and answering questions. You could set a timer to ensure pace, and give rewards such as raffle tickets or house points for excellent pronunciation.

Teaching tip

For more information about Kagan Structures, see www.kaganonline.com.

Taking it further

Tell students what they're going to be doing the lesson before, to allow them time to practise and perfect their question and answer.

Bonus idea ★

Once they're in order, you could ask students to give information about other members of the class, asking them the question and allowing them to respond in the third person, again in the target language.

Talking frames

'How can I help students who are reluctant to take part in speaking activities?'

This is a useful method of supporting student discussions in the target language.

For me, speaking has always been the trickiest skill to teach. A successful speaking activity often requires a lot of preparation, and with a difficult class, students can easily go off-topic, particularly if the activity is not thoroughly planned and thought-through. Those students who lack confidence in their speaking abilities may also easily go off-task. Speaking spontaneously doesn't just come overnight. It's a skill that needs to be practised and developed over time. Talking frames are a way of guiding students and building up their confidence.

Prepare a talking frame in advance. This should show a grid containing questions and possible answers in the target language. On the topic of 'food and drink', for example, the grid could include columns for time phrases, verbs, foods and drinks, and connectives with opinion phrases.

¿Qué desayunas?			
Normalmente	desayuno me gusta desayunar	fruta cereales	porque es deliciosa.
Todos los días			porque es sana.
A veces			porque es rica.
Los fines de semana			porque son deliciosos.
			porque son sanos.
			porque son ricos.

Students can work in pairs, taking it in turns to ask each other and answer the questions by picking a word/phrase from each of the columns. They can extend their answers further if they feel confident to do so.

Chatty Jenga®

'Get students excited about speaking in the target language.'

Combine student discussion with a game of Jenga® to add a competitive element.

Divide students into groups and give each group a Jenga® pack with the blocks numbered, and a sheet of numbered questions in the target language. The students take it in turns to remove a block, asking and answering the corresponding question orally in the target language. Meanwhile, you go round listening to the students' pronunciation and praising those who are working well and giving particularly good answers.

An example game would go as follows:
Player 1 removes a block and reads out the number on it: 'Número diez.'
Player 2 finds the corresponding number on the sheet of questions and reads it out: '¿Qué te gusta hacer en tu tiempo libre?'
Player 1 responds to the question in the target language: 'En mi tiempo libre prefiero leer en mi habitación porque es relajante.'
The other members of the group race to translate the answer into English. Player 2 then removes a piece, with Player 3 asking them the question, and so on.

If the player can provide an answer to the question, they earn ten points. However, if they are unable to, teammates have the opportunity to steal and attempt an answer. If another player can successfully give the answer, they win five points instead. If another player can translate the answer, they win five points. If the tower collapses when a player removes a block, they lose ten points. A trustworthy student in each group will need to keep a tally of the points.

Teaching tip

Make a note of any words that are being mispronounced and practise these with the class once the activity is over.

Taking it further

Include questions from just one topic to make this activity easier, or include questions from multiple topics to increase the challenge.

Speaking survey

'How can I build students' confidence when doing speaking activities?'

One way to encourage pupil talk in the target language is by getting your students to conduct a survey. These are quick to prepare and easily adaptable to suit different classes and topics.

Taking it further

This idea can provide a cross-curricular opportunity, as students could practise their numeracy skills by figuring out percentages (and translating these into the target language) and producing bar charts.

Introduce the vocabulary of the topic you are covering, with plenty of drilling and repetition of the key phrases. Tell your students they will be carrying out a survey and ask them to translate some key questions into the target language. For example, if the topic is 'food and drink', students could ask their classmates what they prefer to eat and drink for breakfast. You could make this either open-ended or multiple choice, by providing students with a grid with the different foods and drinks listed at the top. Next give them a few minutes to prepare their own answers to the questions.

To keep up the pace and stop students standing around in groups talking about who did what on last night's *Love Island*, ask them to spread out across the room. When you clap your hands they must find a partner and will have a minute to ask each other the questions, answer them and fill in their grids. They could do a tally or write their classmates' initials in the different columns. When the minute is up they have to swap and speak to someone else. Repeat a few more times. They will have to repeat similar answers and questions each time, but this repetition will help them to remember the vocabulary.

At the end of the activity, ask students to report back to you with their findings. This is a good opportunity for them to practise using the third person in the target language: 'A Dominic le gusta desayunar cereales, pero Stacey prefiere desayunar tostadas con mermelada.'

Registration conversation

'Registration is a great chance to get students used to asking and answering questions through regular practice.'

This idea was inspired by my esteemed ex-colleague Michèle Lefebvre-Smith, and is a way of developing pupil talk and their confidence to ask questions in the target language.

I remember how I felt the first time I had to stand up and impart wisdom to a class of 30 bloodthirsty teenagers (just kidding – there were only 29). Quite honestly, I was unbelievably nervous, but I got back up and did it again a few more times and eventually I became used to it. The pre-lesson nerves stopped and it became second nature to me. The same goes for students when they are speaking another language. The more regularly they practise it, the easier and less daunting it will become for them. The repetition of using and hearing similar vocabulary each lesson will lead to increased confidence.

This idea works better with smaller classes and can be adapted for any ability or year group. When completing the register, instead of responding with 'Yes Miss/Sir', students have to ask you a question in the target language. This could be anything from a simple 'How are you?' or 'What is your name?' to 'What did you do at the weekend?' or even 'What would you do if you won the lottery?' You will find that the variety of questions asked will broaden throughout the year, as more topics get covered and students are introduced to new vocabulary. With a larger class you could select some students to ask you a question each lesson – simply hand out cards with question marks on to a few students as they are entering the room.

Teaching tip

Students could keep a list of questions in their exercise books that they can add to throughout the year.

Bonus idea ★

As students enter your classroom, hold up a mini whiteboard with a question in the target language. Students can be thinking of an answer while they are getting settled, then share their answer as their name is called during the register.

Lollipop stick phrases

'How can I get my students used to using the target language comfortably and spontaneously?'

This idea encourages spontaneous pupil talk in the target language and rewards those who use it appropriately.

Teaching tip

It may be useful to think of phrases your class say regularly in English and translate these into the target language for them.

This is a way of adding an extra element of challenge to a lesson. Prepare some lollipop sticks with phrases written on in the target language, along with their English translations. These phrases should be useful vocabulary used regularly in your lessons. Each lollipop stick should have a different word or phrase written on it.

You may wish to use some of the following examples:

- How are you?
- Thank you.
- Please.
- Of course.
- See you next week/ tomorrow/later.
- Bless you! (After a sneeze)
- Can you repeat, please?
- How do you say... in... ?
- What is the date?
- The date is the...
- I have a question.

- I've finished.
- I need help.
- I can help.
- That's correct.
- That's wrong.
- Cheat!
- It's my turn.
- I have won.
- I have lost.
- I understand.
- I don't understand.
- I know.
- I don't know.
- Can I hand out/ collect the books?

Bonus idea ★

Ask pupils to teach a friend or family member their phrase as part of their homework.

When students enter the classroom at the start of the lesson, they each take a lollipop stick from the pot. The aim is for students to use their word or phrase in context at some point throughout the lesson. If they use it successfully, they put their stick back in the pot and can be rewarded.

Einundzwanzig

'This is one of my favourite activities to use when teaching numbers.'

I'm a firm believer in the idea that the start of the lesson is the best time to engage your students. Get them hooked at the beginning with a challenging starter activity and they'll be putty in your hands. This speaking activity will do just that.

Ask the class to stand in a circle. They take it in turns to say either one, two or three consecutive numbers in the target language, starting at one and going up to 21. When a player says '21', they are out of the game and must sit down. If they hesitate or make a mistake, they are also out and must sit down.

Once students have played this a few times, you can add an extra challenge. If a student says one number, the person to their left goes next. If a student says two numbers, this reverses the direction, so the player to the right must go next instead. If a player says three numbers, they skip a person. Students are not allowed to say the same amount of numbers as the previous player, as if they keep saying two numbers this will reverse the direction every time so that the same students are taking part.

Another variation of this game is to display some images on the screen or give students a printed copy. The images could be of animals, foods, countries, school subjects – anything related to the topic you are currently covering or even a topic covered previously. Ask students to stand up and look at the images on the board. They take it in turns saying the word in the target language for either one, two or three of the images on the board, starting at the top left. The student who is forced to say the word for the last image on the board is out of the game and must sit down.

Teaching tip

All three variations of this activity can be played in smaller groups as well as being a whole-class exercise.

Speaking ladders

'This adds an element of competition to a speaking activity.'

This game involves students translating sentences orally while moving their counters up the ladder and racing their partner to the top. Many thanks again to Kayleigh Meyrick (@MissMeyMFL) for sharing this superb speaking idea.

Teaching tip

Ask students to make a note of any words they keep forgetting and collate these at the end of the lesson. You could upload this vocabulary to Memrise (see Idea 71) or create a Kahoot quiz (see Idea 78) to help them practise these words independently outside of the lesson.

Prepare two different sheets before the lesson, each with 15 sentences in the target language on the left-hand side and the English translations next to them on the right (see the online resources for an example). Start with simple sentences at the bottom, which progressively become more difficult as you move towards the top, e.g. by introducing connectives, justified opinions and a range of tenses.

Students work in pairs, with one given sheet A and the other sheet B. Ask students to cover up the English side, then read through the sentences, highlighting any words they don't know, allowing you to see any gaps in their knowledge.

Provide each student with a printed-out image of a ladder with 15 steps. Each step represents one of the 15 sentences. Give every student a counter, which they place on the first step of the ladder. Player A reads the first sentence out loud (starting from the bottom) and Player B tries to translate it. Player A can check the answer on their own sheet. If the student is correct, they move their counter to the next step. They then swap roles and repeat.

When a student translates a sentence incorrectly, they fall to the bottom of the ladder and have to start again. The winner is the first student to reach the top of the ladder. The game can be replayed by translating sentences from English into the target language.

Topic talk

'This exercise works well in the run-up to any speaking exams, once all the relevant topics have been covered and you are confident your students know the vocabulary.'

This is an activity in which students are asked to speak at length on a particular topic.

Prepare some cards with topics written on them. Invite a student to stand at the front of the class. You could use a random name generator for this. The student chooses a card at random from the pile. Display a stopwatch on the board and ask the student to aim to speak about the topic for one minute. The timings can be shorter or longer depending on the level of the class. When the student has finished speaking, ask the other students to say what went well, e.g. 'You spoke clearly and confidently', and how they could improve, e.g. 'You could include another tense'. With a more able class, the other students could ask them questions in the target language.

Once this has been modelled for the class, students can repeat the activity in pairs. They take it in turns, with one choosing a card and speaking about a topic for a minute and the student giving constructive feedback and asking questions in the target language.

At the end of the activity, give students some time to reflect on what they are finding easy and what they need to spend more time revising before the exams. Students could set themselves a SMART target, saying what they are going to do in order to improve in this area, e.g. 'I really struggled to speak in detail about the environment. I will revise the environment vocabulary using Memrise and complete this by Friday 15th.' It may be useful to keep a record of these targets and regularly check up on progress.

> **Teaching tip**
>
> Provide students with a talking frame (see Idea 3) to support them with this.

11

Trapdoor

'One of my all-time favourite MFL activities!'

This is an excellent game that utilises not only students' speaking skills but reading and listening too.

Students are shown some sentences in the target language, with each sentence containing several possible options. These can be displayed on the board. Choose each of the options randomly and the students then try to guess which ones you have selected.

Here is a shortened example in German:

Manchmal gehe ich mit meinem Vater (ins Kino/einkaufen/schwimmen), weil es lustig ist. Jeden Tag spiele ich mit (meiner Schwester/meinem Bruder/meiner Mutter) Fußball aber es ist anstrengend.

One student starts by reading the first sentence out loud. If they successfully guess the first option, they continue reading until they get one wrong. If they guess incorrectly, invite another student to read from the beginning, and so on until a student is able to get to the end of the paragraph by guessing all of the options correctly.

As the aim of the game is to reach the end of the paragraph by reading out the correct option in each sentence, students have to listen carefully to each other and are therefore unlikely to become distracted. They don't want to repeat an answer someone has already said if it is wrong. One reason I love this activity is that the repetition helps the students to remember these key phrases. It also allows the teacher to pick up on any mispronunciations.

Many thanks to Stuart Gorse (@gorsey) for the inspiration for this idea.

The big debate

'I think the key to a successful debate, particularly in MFL, is giving your students enough time to thoroughly prepare.'

Students debate a controversial topic in the target language.

As a starter activity, provide students with a picture prompt. This should be an image representing a particularly controversial topic. It could be relating to technology, social media, smoking, drugs or alcohol, for example – anything that encourages a range of opinions. This could be displayed on the board or printed off, with one copy per group. Allow students some time to brainstorm ideas, vocabulary and arguments relating to that topic in English. A more able group could do this part of the exercise in the target language. Students can then share these ideas with the rest of the class.

Now show the class a statement in the target language. Divide the class into two halves – one side agrees with the statement and the other does not. Give students time in groups to prepare their arguments, to think about what the opposition could say, and how they could respond to it in the target language. If the class is small, you could allocate each student a 'character', so they can focus on producing specific arguments from a particular person's point of view. One of my groups once debated 'Technology – is it a good or a bad thing?' and I had a student, a librarian, a parent and a teacher, among others. You may also wish to provide each group with some arguments in English and ask them to translate these. Ask students to learn their arguments off by heart and practise the pronunciation. When it is time for the debate, remind students to speak clearly and confidently, and allow the groups to take it in turns to put across their side of the argument.

Teaching tip

Provide students with a set of opinion phrases in the target language that they can use during the debate.

Speed dating

'This activity requires whole-class participation, enabling the teacher to circulate the classroom, listening to students' pronunciation and providing extra support where necessary.'

This classic MFL activity is a brilliant way of getting students to practise their speaking exam questions and answers.

Before the lesson you will need to set up a row of desks, with chairs either side in two lines facing each other. Students on one side of each desk should be given a card with some speaking questions written on it in the target language, along with success criteria that they can use as a checklist. Try to give some students the same questions and some different, so that when the other students are answering the questions they are encountering a variety of topics, but also repeating certain questions. This repetition will help students to become more confident and fluent in their answers. Students on the other side of the desk should practise answering the questions in the target language.

Five minutes each should be enough time to answer a couple of questions and receive feedback from their 'date' on what went well and how they could improve their answers. Once the five minutes are up, the students answering the questions should move around the room clockwise to their next 'date'. After a few rounds, ask students to swap roles so that the students who previously asked the questions and gave feedback are now answering them instead.

> **Bonus idea** ★
>
> Alternatively, you could use this activity as a way of preparing your students for the role-play element of the speaking exam, an idea shared by Kayleigh Meyrick (@MissMeyMFL) on her fantastic blog. Simply provide half of your students with copies of the role play cards and the other half with the teacher instructions. For more information visit Kayleigh's blog: https://missmeymfl.wordpress.com.

Tongue twisters

'I like to use tongue twisters as a warm-up activity before another speaking activity. They are a fun way to boost speaking skills and practise different sounds.'

Tongue twisters are a light-hearted, zero-pressure way of allowing students to practise their speaking skills and perfect their accent, while learning that it's okay to make mistakes.

In order to develop student confidence when speaking in the target language and to develop their speaking skills, it's important to create a classroom atmosphere in which students feel comfortable to have a go and not feel embarrassed if they make a mistake. Tongue twisters are a great way of doing this. Students have so much fun trying to pronounce the silly sentences that they tend to forget they are speaking in the target language.

Before the lesson, choose the tongue twisters you want your students to practise or ask your students to research and bring in their own for homework. Students then practise reading out the tongue twisters, getting faster each time until they can say them quickly from memory.

A fun alternative is to combine this with a quick game of Chinese whispers. Put students in groups and number them one to five, for example. Student 1 from each group comes to you to listen to the pronunciation of the tongue twister, which they will read to Student 2, and so on. Ask each student at the end to say the tongue twister, and reward the group with the best pronunciation.

Teaching tip

You can find tongue twisters in a range of languages on Rachel Hawkes' website (www.rachelhawkes.com/Resources/Phonics/Phonics.php), or there are videos with the pronunciation on YouTube, e.g. www.youtube.com/watch?v=EgViNp2ZqFQ&t=55s.

Bonus idea ★

A fun idea as part of European Languages Week is to run a tongue twister competition. Students can spend time in the lesson practising some target language tongue twisters, then make a poster showing their favourite one. The winner could receive a prize and the best, most creative posters will make a lovely display for the MFL department.

Listening

Part 2

Dictation drawing

'How can I get my students excited about listening activities?'

A nice, low-stakes listening exercise that invites a bit of creativity.

Either play a recording or read out a prepared text and, if possible, provide each student with a mini whiteboard and pen. Instead of answering questions or writing what they hear, the students just draw a picture of it. You may need to play the recording or read it out several times to give them time to draw. You should find that your students generally feel quite positive about this activity. As they aren't restricted to answering certain questions, this really takes the pressure off. It also allows students to be quite creative with their drawings.

For example, for this sentence in a recording about a person's daily routine, 'A las siete de la mañana me lavo los dientes antes de vestirme', students could draw a clock showing 7:00 am, a toothbrush and an item of clothing.

Once you've finished reading out the text or playing the recording, ask students to compare their drawings with the person next to them and discuss in pairs what they understood. You can then ask the class to feed back to you, either in English or in the target language, depending on the ability of your students. To add an extra challenge, students could provide their feedback using the third person.

Bonus idea ★

Provide students with the transcript and this could double-up as a reading activity.

Play that funky music

'Can we listen to music, Miss?'

Students often ask me whether they can listen to music in lessons, so I have come up with ideas for incorporating songs into the lesson in a way that will help students to improve their listening skills. Below are several exercises that can be used alongside songs in the target language. There is a vast array of foreign language songs available on YouTube and Spotify.

Gap fill: Students listen to the song, look at the lyrics with words missing and fill in the gaps. The missing words or the first letter of each of the missing words could be given to students who are struggling to complete the task.

Comprehension: Students listen to the song and answer questions about it, either in English or the target language.

Finding examples: Students listen to the song and write down (or highlight, if they are given the printed-off lyrics) examples of a particular tense – for example, the Beyoncé song 'If I Were a Boy' translated into Spanish ('Si Yo Fuera Un Chico') could be used when practising the imperfect subjunctive with the conditional.

Order it: Students listen to the song with lyrics printed on cards and put these in the correct order.

Bad lyrics: Students are given the lyrics printed off with a few mistakes and have to highlight the words that are incorrect. As an extra challenge, they could write the correct words above.

Teaching tip

Websites such as www.lyricstraining.com have songs in a variety of languages and allow students to listen to a song and fill in the gaps in the target language. This website in particular has songs in a range of languages, including French, Spanish, German, Italian, Japanese and Polish, and is suitable for all language learners, from beginners to expert level.

Positive, negative or both?

'This technique reminds students to listen to the whole recording when completing a listening exercise.'

For this exercise, students listen to a recording in which several people give their opinions on a particular topic. Students then have to decide whether each of the statements is positive, negative or both.

One issue we sometimes encounter with this type of activity is that when students hear a word such as 'aburrido' (boring) in Spanish, they automatically stop listening to the rest of the recording and write down 'negative' as their answer. The technique below can be used for this sort of activity in class, but it can also help pupils in their listening exams if used properly.

First, ask students to read the question carefully and highlight any key words, e.g. 'Listen to these four people describing their town and decide whether each person's opinion is positive (P), negative (N) or both (PN).' They then draw a grid similar to the one on the left (a printable version can be downloaded from the online resources).

Give students time in the lesson before they listen to the recording to discuss what positive and negative town-related statements they might hear. Students may wish to make a note of these below each of the columns in their grid. For example, they could write *limpio* (clean), *bonito* (pretty) and *hay mucho que hacer* (there is lots to do) underneath the positive column, and *aburrido* (boring), *sucio* (dirty) and *contaminación* (pollution) underneath the negative column.

Positive	Negative
Q1	
Q2	
Q3	
Q4	

While listening to the recording, students simply tick the P column if they hear something positive and the N column if they hear something negative. If both boxes are ticked, they know the answer is PN.

Actions

'Not only does this activity provide students with an opportunity to hear the pronunciation of important vocabulary, but it also gets them focused and actively reading the text.'

This kinaesthetic activity is great for those reluctant listeners and is a nice way of seeing which students are paying attention.

I generally like to do this activity before a reading comprehension exercise to allow students to familiarise themselves with the content before answering questions about it. Students listen to a recording in the target language while reading the transcript. They then do certain actions when they come across particular elements of the text – for example, clapping when they reach a full stop, clicking their fingers when they see a verb and raising their hand when they come across an accent. You decide the actions and write these up on the board as a reminder at the start of the activity.

With more advanced students, they could be looking out for verbs in the present, past and future tense, or verbs, connectives and adverbs of time. They could then be allocated some time to read through the text again and highlight these elements in different colours, before answering some reading comprehension questions (see Idea 30).

By doing this exercise, students are actively involved in their learning, instead of just pretending to listen to the recording as they sometimes do. It also enables you to check that students are capable of recognising the words they hear and following the text.

Taking it further

With an advanced class, you could do this activity without the transcript. Students have to listen carefully and identify verbs and do a particular action depending on whether the tense is the present, past or future.

Life abroad

'I find this is an excellent way of developing positive relationships with your students, and shows them you do indeed have a life outside of the four walls of the classroom.'

Don't be afraid to share your own experiences with your students. Some of them may have never set foot outside of their own town, never mind travelled abroad.

When covering the 'holidays' topic, my pupils loved hearing about my trip to Peru. I showed them photos of the time I spent in the Amazon jungle and completing the Inca Trail to Machu Picchu. While learning about festivals, I told my students about my year abroad as part of my degree and how I was lucky to experience Las Fallas and La Noche de San Juan during my six months in Valencia. It's important to make sure students are aware of the opportunities available to them if they can speak a second language. Sharing these experiences also expands their understanding of other cultures and broadens their horizons.

Students can then make notes in English showing what they have understood, as well as writing down any new target language they hear. With a confident group, you can ask them questions at the end, which they can respond to in the target language.

Additionally, ask staff in your school to share their own travel and language experiences and photos with you. You can then collate their responses to make a display in your department. Students will be fascinated to read about how the head of PE spent six months in Japan learning the language or how an LSA grew up in France and can speak French fluently. This is a nice way to raise the profile of MFL in your school and will show how useful languages can be.

Bonus idea ★

YouTube has a variety of cultural videos available on different topics and in a range of languages. Provide students with a transcript with missing words and ask them to fill in the gaps while listening and watching the video.

Directions

'This is a great activity that gives students the chance to use and hear some transactional language.'

This exercise provides an opportunity for students to develop their speaking and listening skills by giving and understanding directions in the target language.

There are several versions of this activity, but they are all best used after you have introduced the vocabulary for places in a town, directions and prepositions and only when you feel students are confident with the language.

Version 1: Students are given a map of a town. Listening carefully to you, they have to follow directions given in the target language, then say what place they end up at on the map. This could be done as a race; the first student to put their hand up and say the correct place in the target language could win a prize. Repeat this several times, with a different finish point each time.

Version 2: The activity could also be done in pairs as a combined speaking and listening activity. Provide each student with sentences to read out in the target language (these should be different to their partner's), while their partner follows the directions to find the destination.

Version 3: Prepare two different maps showing places in a town and ask students to work in pairs. Student 1 has a copy of Map A with some places missing and Map B, which is complete. Student 2 has Map B with some places missing and the complete Map A. Remind students to hide their completed maps from their partners so that no cheating can occur. They take it in turns to ask each other where the missing places are and fill in the gaps on their own map.

Teaching tip

With a smaller, younger group, a children's road map play mat and some toy cars could also work well combined with some of these exercises!

Mini whiteboard dictation

'A highly effective listening activity using mini whiteboards.'

Dictation exercises have been around for years and, despite having a bit of a bad reputation, they are still used by many teachers today in the MFL classroom – and they work!

I like to do dictation activities using the mini whiteboards as this allows me to check the understanding of all of my students easily and efficiently. I can give students instant feedback while it's all fresh in their minds and, as an added bonus, it helps to cut down on marking!

Firstly, provide each student with a mini whiteboard and a whiteboard pen, then simply read out a word, phrase or sentence in the target language. Students try to write down what they hear on their boards. You will probably have to repeat the phrases a few times, and may need to break sentences down into smaller chunks to give students enough time to write. Remind students to write the words big and neat enough for you to be able to read them from across the classroom. When you think all students have finished, ask them to hold up their boards so you can see their answers.

A pre-prepared PowerPoint could have the correct answers on individual slides to enable the students to self-mark or swap boards with their partner and peer-assess. When marking their work, ensure that students check every single word. I've found that asking them to tick each word helps them to really focus on the accuracy of each word.

This activity could also be made into a competition by making each word worth a certain amount of points, depending on the word's complexity. If the student has written down the word correctly, they get the points. The student with the most points could win a prize.

I also like to hold up a few student examples, both correct and incorrect ones, as this allows us to focus on particular grammatical aspects and is a really good way to improve the accuracy of students' work.

For example, if you read out the following sentence: 'Hier ma sœur est allée au cinéma', a student may write 'Hier ma sœur est allé au cinéma.' The following conversation (or something along these lines, depending on the ability of your students) could then take place:

Teacher: 'What is good about this answer?'

Student: 'They have remembered the accents on *allé* and *cinéma*, and they have spelt *sœur* correctly.'

Teacher: 'Could it be improved?'

Student: 'The word *allé* needs an extra e.'

Teacher: 'Why?'

Student: 'Because *aller* is an *être* verb in the perfect tense, and needs to agree. *Sœur* means sister so *allé* needs an extra e to make it feminine.'

Taking it further

Make a note of any students who are repeatedly getting answers wrong. Jamie Johnson (@MissJDA24) invites struggling students to her 'Languages Clinic' to receive some extra support. She sends postcards home to invite specific students to attend to help address weaknesses.

Describing photos

'How can I prepare my students for the photocard element of the GCSE exam?'

This listening activity is particularly useful for any students sitting an exam in which they have to describe an image. It gets them used to the vocabulary they will need to use for this.

Teaching tip

A quick search on Google Images will bring up plenty of resources you could use for this activity.

In this game, students could work individually or could compete against other players in their group. Give students a set of printed-out images and ask them to spread these out across their desk. You then read out a description of one of the cards and students have to listen carefully and then hold up the correct photo. If students are working in groups for this exercise, they will need to race the other players in the group to be the first one to find and hold up the correct card.

With beginners, this could be done with individual words. For example, if you have been learning about clothes, you could simply print out some pictures of different items of clothing. With more advanced students, you could provide them with several more detailed images, e.g. images of bedrooms, and read out full descriptions until the students have found the correct one. Several similar images would work well for this; otherwise, the answer may be too obvious. After each round, ask students to feed back to you what they think you said, as this will allow you to check that they haven't just seen and copied another student's answer.

What's next?

'The students have to think carefully about sentence structure and identify what kinds of words fit together.'

This is a competitive game in which students listen to sentence starters and then have to write down what could come next.

Before the lesson, make sure you have some sentences prepared in the target language. These sentences should be relevant to what you are currently covering in class. In the lesson, give each student a mini whiteboard and pen. Ask them all to stand up and make sure they are listening carefully, then read out the first part of one of your sentences. Give students time to finish off the sentence on their mini whiteboards. The aim of the game is to come up with an accurate ending that fits the sentence, but which is different to the sentence you have prepared.

For example, if you say, 'Je joue au...' the students could write 'foot', 'basket', 'tennis' or any other masculine ball sport. Students hold up their boards while you read out the full sentence. If you then say, 'Je joue au foot', any students who have written 'foot' are out of the game and sit down. Equally, if a student writes 'natation', they are also out of the game as the sentence would not make sense.

If you then read out the phrase, 'Je lis un livre dans le...', the students could write 'jardin' or 'salon'. Any student who has the same answer as you is out of the game. Likewise, if a student has written 'cuisine' they are also out, as this would be grammatically inaccurate.

Repeat these steps several times and give out a prize(s) to the last student(s) standing.

Teaching tip

Once you have played this as a class a few times, students could play it in groups, with one student reading out the starts of sentences and the other group members trying to come up with alternative endings.

Vocab bingo

'I like to use bingo as a way of developing my students' listening skills.'

This is a fun way to check whether students can recognise and translate new vocabulary in its spoken form.

Students will need to draw a quick 3 x 3 grid in their books. Alternatively, you could have these prepared and printed off ready for students before the lesson. Ask your students to write in nine words or phrases from the current topic in English and hide their sheets from their neighbour. To save time in the lesson, you may wish to have these grids filled in ready for your students; however, each student would need a different grid, so it may take some time to prepare.

When the students have prepared their bingo grids, you call out relevant words in the target language, while students listen carefully and cross through any translations that they have written on their sheets. The first student to get three in a row is the winner. Next you can play for a full house.

Make a note of the vocabulary you call out as you go along and then get the winner to read out their answers to check they haven't misheard and crossed out a word incorrectly.

Bonus idea ★

Bingo is a great game to play when practising numbers. You can buy books of bingo tickets cheaply in the UK from shops such as Wilko. Just call out the numbers in the target language while students cross these out on their sheets.

Picture perfect

'This works particularly well when learning the vocabulary for items in a house or places in a town and prepositions.'

Students work in pairs, developing their speaking and listening skills by taking it in turns describing an image to their partner, who has to listen to the description and draw it based on what they have heard.

Ask students to sit back to back, with one of them facing the board and the other facing away. Then display an image on the board – this could be an image of a town or a bedroom, for example. Set a timer for around two minutes (or less or more, depending on the image you have chosen and the ability of your students). The student facing the board describes the image the best they can in the target language, while their partner draws a picture based on their description. This could be done in books or on mini whiteboards. When the timer is up, ask students to turn around and face the board so that they can compare what they have drawn with the image on the board. You can circulate the classroom at this point and look at the drawings. This will allow you to see where there are gaps in your students' knowledge. Perhaps the same item is missing from every student's drawing. This shows you which vocabulary will need to be revisited. Students can then swap roles and repeat the steps for a different image.

A variation is to display a text on the board instead of an image. Again, students sit back to back, with one dictating and the other writing down exactly what they hear or making notes and taking down any key information in English. This excellent activity enables students to develop their reading, listening, speaking and writing skills all in one go.

Teaching tip

A talking frame (see Idea 3) may be useful for less able students, to support their speaking.

Reading

Part 3

The detectives

'A fantastic reading activity that can be used with complete beginners or advanced learners.'

This is a useful reading activity, which also acts as an alternative method of introducing new vocabulary.

Taking it further

Students could then be given sentences including some of these phrases to translate into the target language, before producing their own piece of writing in which they could try to incorporate the new vocabulary they have learned.

Students read through a text in the target language and are given a list of English words or phrases to find in the text. They could copy the translations below the text next to the English phrase. Alternatively, they can simply highlight the phrases in the text in different colours, with the English translations highlighted in the same colours to make them easy to find later on.

For example, part of a text could be: 'Je m'appelle Yasmine et j'ai quinze ans. J'habite à Manchester avec ma mère et mon frère et j'adore jouer au rugby.' Students could be asked to find the phrases 'my name is', 'I am... years old', 'I live' and 'I love to play'. They will be able to recognise Manchester, so should be able to figure out that 'J'habite' means 'I live'.

For more advanced learners, a text discussing the advantages and disadvantages of technology could include the following sentence: 'Le week-end je préfère jouer aux jeux-vidéos, mais c'est une perte de temps.' Students are then asked to find the phrase 'but it's a waste of time'. They may know the French word for 'but', which will help them to locate the rest of the phrase within the text. It could be that students already know one word from the phrase and are therefore able to figure out the remainder, or they may be able to guess it from context. If students are finding this too tricky, they could be given the first letter of each word in the phrase to help them. For example: but it's a waste of time = m c u p d t.

Heads and tails sentences

'This activity is great for practising grammar, as students are required to think about what types of words need to go together.'

This is a helpful way of encouraging students to think carefully about word order and sentence structure.

Provide students with a sheet of sentence starters and ends that can be matched up to make full sentences. First, ask them to translate and annotate as much of the vocabulary as possible. You can discuss this as a class and decide what types of words they are.

Students should then read through the first part of each sentence and consider what type of word could follow it, e.g. after 'c'est' it could be an adjective (e.g. nul) or a noun (e.g. une perte de temps). An opinion phrase or justification is likely to follow 'parce que' or 'car'. Students should then decide which sentence end contains the correct type of word or phrase and matches up with the first part of each sentence.

Alternatively, the sentences could be printed off and cut up into cards, which students then have to match together. It may be worth laminating them, so that you can use them again in future with other classes.

Teaching tip

For less able students or beginners, this exercise could be done with individual words by splitting them in half and asking students to match up the beginning of each word to its correct ending.

Bonus idea ★

Use this exercise if you need to get your students in pairs. Give each student a card with the beginning or end of a sentence. They circulate the room reading out their part of the sentence until they find their partner with the card that completes the sentence.

Active reading

'My students really enjoyed the challenge, as well as the opportunity to be independent and actively take ownership of their learning.'

This is a great way to develop your students' reading skills, while also introducing them to new vocabulary.

Taking it further

Display some other images of celebrities without their descriptions. If students fill in their grid quickly, invite them to use this vocabulary to add their own descriptions of these celebrities to the speech bubbles.

I have used this idea when covering the topic of 'appearance' in a lesson on physical descriptions, but it could easily be adapted for other topics. Before the lesson, prepare some sheets with images of celebrities and speech bubbles containing physical descriptions, detailing their hairstyles and eye colours in the target language. I find this activity works best if the majority of the vocabulary is completely new to students. Stick these sheets up around the room, then provide each of the students with a vocabulary grid with the English column filled in and the majority of the translations missing, ready for the students to fill in.

This activity gives students the opportunity to practise writing out the new spellings, as they are given a set amount of time to circulate the room with their sheet and a pen, find all of the celebrities and note down the key vocabulary in their grid. The key vocabulary can be underlined in the descriptions to make it easier.

Example:

English	Español
I have... (adjective)... hair	Tengo el pelo... (adjective)
...long ...	
...short ...	
...red ...	

Quickly go over these phrases as a class, practising the pronunciation and allowing students time to correct any errors.

Reading relay

'A running dictation activity with a bit of a twist.'

Use this challenging and active reading exercise when students need waking up on a Monday morning or to use up a bit of energy after lunch.

Firstly, you will need to prepare a text relevant to the topic currently being studied. Print off several copies and stick these up on the wall around the classroom. You will also need to provide a sheet of questions about the text – it would be a good idea to have at least one question per sentence. The questions could be in English or the target language, depending on the ability of your group.

Put students into groups of four and number them one to four. Provide each group with a mini whiteboard, a whiteboard pen and a question sheet.

Student number one from each group goes to one of the sheets on the wall and has one minute to read and memorise as much of the text as possible. During this first minute, the other three members of the group should read through the questions and highlight in the questions the key things they should be looking for. When the minute is up, student number one returns to their group. They then have another minute to dictate as much of the text as they can remember, while student number two scribes and students three and four start writing down the answers to the questions about the text. They continue to take it in turns to run up to their allocated text and memorise it in the set amount of time, before returning to their table and answering as many questions as possible (see Idea 30 for reading comprehension ideas).

Teaching tip

Foreign news websites are a good place for sourcing authentic, relevant and up-to-date reading comprehension texts.

Read all about it

'How can I properly prepare my students for the reading exam?'

Regular practice of exam-style reading questions is key to developing student confidence and effective comprehension skills.

Provide students with something relevant to read in the target language, whether this is a paragraph from a textbook or even a newspaper article – you don't always have to prepare a text from scratch. Textbooks and the *TES* website, among others, offer a whole host of ready-written texts. You could even adapt texts from past papers. Then give the students a range of questions to gauge their understanding of the text. Below are some suggestions for suitable types of question:

Either/or?

What school subject does Felipe dislike the most – English or French?

Students simply choose one of the two options.

Multiple choice

How does Jacob travel to school – by car, by bus or by foot?

Students could translate each of the options into the target language beforehand, then search for these words within the text.

Multiple correct answers

Tick three fruits that Lily says she likes: bananas, pears, apples, strawberries, raspberries, melon, oranges.

Make students aware that Lily could mention fruits she dislikes or fruits her friend likes. Students should be encouraged to read all the choices before making their selection.

True/false

Selma lives with her grandparents.

Students simply have to decide whether the statement is true or false. Encourage students to read the text carefully and beware of questions like this. Selma could say that she lives near her grandparents, or that she wishes she lived with her grandparents, in which case the answer would be 'false'.

Who... ?

Who says they are keen to go to university when they're older?

Students could be given statements from three different people and have to decide which one said a particular thing.

Open-ended questions

What does Marie think of the public transport in her area? (1)

Why does Matthew say he does not want to get married? Give two reasons. (2)

What happened when Samira's parents returned from their holiday? (3)

List three advantages and three disadvantages that Deepash gives for living in the countryside. (6)

Train students to look at the number in brackets to know how many points the question is worth and therefore how many bits of information they need to give.

Students could be given the questions before the text and asked to consider what information they'll need to look out for. Encourage students to read the questions carefully and underline or highlight any key words in the questions. Some students may find it useful to highlight the answers in the text.

> **Bonus idea**
>
> The same text can be used for a listening activity, perhaps before it is used as a reading comprehension exercise. You read the text out loud, while students listen and read through the text. You can pause at certain points and choose individual students or the whole class to say the next word.

Break it up

'I like to use this as a starter activity in order to check how well the students have retained the spellings of vocabulary from previous lessons.'

This is a simple reading activity that gets students carefully considering spellings of vocabulary.

Taking it further

As an extension challenge, ask your students to change a detail in each sentence or extend it. For example: 'Mi asignatura preferida es el inglés porque me da la oportunidad de ser creativo', 'Me mola el dibujo porque me da la oportunidad de ser creativo' or 'Mi asignatura preferida es el dibujo dado que me da la oportunidad de ser creativo.'

Display some sentences on the board that appear as one long word without gaps, or give each student their own individual printed-out copy. Students are then given a set amount of time to separate the words. You could ask them to rewrite each sentence, putting the gaps in the correct places, or to simply draw a line in between each word.

Alternatively, give each student a different sentence and a pair of scissors and ask them to cut up each individual word. You could tell your students that this has to be completed by the time you've finished the register and reward the student who finishes first.

Here's an example:

Question: 'Miasignaturapre feridaeseldibujoporque medalaoportunidaddesercreativo.'

Answer: 'Mi asignatura preferida es el dibujo porque me da la oportunidad de ser creativo.'

When the students have successfully separated the words in all of the sentences, they should write the translations underneath in English.

Exploiting texts

'Don't reinvent the wheel.'

There is no need to create several different texts for one lesson. The same text can be used for a range of activities.

There are a ton of texts already available online and in textbooks. Lighten your workload by using the same text alongside different exercises in order to get the most out of it. Pick and choose between the following activities and follow these up with some comprehension questions to check the students' understanding (see Idea 30).

Idea 1 – Categorise: Ask students to read through the text, identifying different features within it. They could highlight the verbs in different colours depending on the tense, underline the adjectives, draw a circle around the opinion phrases and draw a box around the time and frequency phrases.

Idea 2 – Reduce: Ask students to summarise each paragraph of the text in their own words. Alternatively, they could add a title to each paragraph – you may wish to provide them with the titles or allow them to create their own.

Idea 3 – Transform: Ask students to change the text from first person to third person. Alternatively, ask students to change the tense, e.g. from the present tense to the past tense.

Idea 4 – Find: Students look for synonyms for a list of words in the target language, for example, 'Find another way of saying "Me gusta"' (Me mola).

Teaching tip

These activities would work well alongside the 'Actions' listening exercise (see Idea 18).

Similar texts

'The repetition of vocabulary helps my students to remember those important phrases.'

This reading exercise is a great one to do just before you set your students a written task.

Prepare two texts, both of which follow a similar structure. Try to use familiar vocabulary and phrases that you would like students to include in their own writing. For example:

| Je m'appelle Margot et j'ai dix-sept ans. J'habite avec mes parents dans la banlieue de Paris. J'adore Paris car il y a beaucoup à faire, mais c'est un peu sale. Si j'avais le choix je préférerais habiter à Bordeaux. | Je m'appelle Jamal. J'ai dix-sept ans et j'habite avec mes copains dans la banlieue de Bordeaux. J'aime Bordeaux car c'est joli, mais il n'y a rien à faire. A l'avenir je voudrais habiter à Paris. J'adore Paris! |

Idea 1: Provide target language sentences about the texts and ask students to decide whether they are true or false. Students could write out the false sentences correctly. This gives them the opportunity to adapt familiar language, as well as practise using the third person:

Margot habite avec ses copains → Faux. Margot habite avec ses parents. Jamal habite avec ses copains.

Idea 2: Provide sentences in English and students have to decide which of the two texts each one is referring to:

I live in the suburbs of Paris. → Margot
It's pretty, but there is nothing to do. → Jamal

Idea 3: Students search for the differences and similarities between two texts.

Similarities: They both love Paris and they are both 17 years old.
Differences: Margot lives in Paris, but Jamal lives in Bordeaux.

Taking it further

Ask students to produce their own paragraph following the same structure used in the two examples above.

Reading for points

'A simple reading comprehension exercise can be jazzed up by adding an element of competition.'

This competitive exercise will ensure that students are really focused when reading a text, and shows you how much your students have understood.

Before the lesson, you will need to create or find a text about the current topic, as well as some questions to go with it. Print off enough copies of the text for one per student. Give students a set amount of time to read through the text. I would get them to do this part of the exercise in silence to ensure that they're really focused on the task. Display a countdown timer on the board. While the timer is counting down, students should be carefully reading through the text and making notes as they go along.

At the end of the allotted time, split the class into two teams and display your prepared questions on the board. Students can have their notes available during this time, but you may wish to ask them to cover up the text. There is a ready-made template for this game in the online resources, but you can easily make your own. Behind each question there should be a number, either a positive or a negative one. This is the amount of points a student will earn for their team if they answer the question correctly. Every time a box is clicked, it disappears and reveals the number behind it.

The questions should be a combination of comprehension questions and translation questions, where students are required to translate certain phrases they will have seen in the text.

Order!

'How can I get my students to engage with a text in the target language?'

This exercise requires students to read through a text carefully and decide the order in which certain things are mentioned.

Before your lesson, prepare or find a text relevant to your current topic. Create some cards showing images relating to certain parts of the text – for example, if the text mentions 'la natation', print off an image of a person swimming. Provide students with a copy of the text, as well as a pack of the cards between two. Students work in pairs and simply read through the text, placing the cards in the order that they appear within it.

Alternatively, you could provide students with a list of topics – these could be synonyms for information given in the text. Students could then state the order in which the topics are mentioned in the text.

For example: State the order in which the following topics are mentioned in the text below.

los deportes acuáticos / la natación / el jogging / los deportes de pelota / el ciclismo

La salud es muy importante para mí. Para mantenerme en forma voy al instituto en bicicleta todos los días. Durante el recreo suelo jugar al tenis o al fútbol con mis compañeros de clase. Los lunes y los viernes tengo clase de educación física donde normalmente hay que ir a correr. Antes de volver a casa me mola pasar una hora en la piscina. Los fines de semana practico la vela o el buceo ya que me encanta estar en el agua.

Bonus idea ★

This could first be done as a listening exercise, in which case allow students to look at the transcript and check that they are happy with their answers before marking it together as a class.

Writing

Part 4

Writing preparation sheet

'It really helps to look at an example so I know what I should be including in my own written work.'

In this exercise, students analyse a text prepared by the teacher to assist them with the planning of their own piece of writing.

Teaching tip

A template for this activity can be found in the online resources.

Taking it further

Provide extra support by including a structure strip alongside this (see Idea 40).

Bonus idea ★

Provide students with a mark scheme and ask them to work together to grade the example. They can give reasons why they think it would achieve this grade and say what they would do to improve it.

Provide students with a sheet with a model text in the target language in the middle and eight boxes around it containing these headings:

- Time phrases
- Past tense verbs
- Other people (verbs in the third person, e.g. other people's opinions)
- Adjectives
- Opinions
- Present tense verbs
- Connectives
- Future tense or conditional verbs

Adding a picture clue to each heading can be a great help – you can use them regularly, displaying them on the board any time students are producing a written piece so that they remember what they need to include in their piece of writing to make it successful. They will learn that the clock symbolises 'time phrases', the smiley face is the symbol for 'opinions' and the jigsaw piece reminds them to include 'connectives'.

Students read through the text and make a note of any examples in the boxes around the side. Alternatively, they could highlight the words or phrases in the text in different colours. Discuss what makes it a successful piece of writing and share ideas as a class.

Provide each student with a blank copy of the sheet and give them time to write in the boxes and plan what adjectives, connectives, etc. they will include in their own writing. They can steal some examples from the model answer, as well as including their own. Students then produce their own piece on the middle of the sheet.

Snowballs

'An exciting activity to get students warmed up in the winter months.'

Getting students to write and enjoy writing can be a challenge, particularly for less able students. This exercise adds an element of fun, while helping students to consider how sentences are structured.

Provide each student with a piece of paper and ask them to write part of a sentence at the top of their sheet – this would depend on the topic you are covering, but it could be an opinion phrase, for example. You may wish to discuss with your class what is meant by an opinion phrase, or have some examples ready on the board. Quickly circulate to check that all pupils have done this, then ask them to screw up their paper and throw it into the middle of the room – or anywhere in the room where there aren't other students and ideally not where you are standing unless you are keen to lose an eye!

Now ask them each to pick up one of the 'snowballs' from the floor, unravel it and add the next part of the sentence – in this case it could be a verb. Repeat the above steps and write who they do the activity with. Repeat again and include a connective. Repeat one more time and give a reason why, including an adjective (they may also be able to include a quantifier).

Each time a student picks up a different snowball they add one new element until there is a full sentence. Finally, students can choose another snowball, check its accuracy, correct any mistakes then translate into English. Students then read out the sentence in the target language, along with the translation, to the class. The rest of the class decide whether the sentence and translation are correct or not.

Teaching tip

Stand by the door with the bin and ask each student to put their snowball in on the way out, to save you picking them up in your breaktime.

Stretching sentences

'How can I help my students include longer, more detailed sentences in their written work?'

Stretching sentences allows students to work in groups, developing and extending sentences provided by the teacher.

Put your students in groups and provide each group with several sheets of A4 paper with one word on each, as well as a few blank sheets (or a mini whiteboard). When put together in the correct order, these words will make a simple sentence relating to the topic you are currently teaching. Each group should have a different sentence. The students have to work together in their groups to figure out the correct order and then stand holding their sentence up in the air.

They should then write extra words on the spare sheets to extend their basic sentence, e.g. by adding an opinion and a justification.

Make this competitive by giving out points for each correctly ordered sentence, as well as extra points for those who have successfully 'stretched their sentences'.

After each completed sentence, when you have checked for accuracy, the students in other groups race to translate the sentence to win bonus points for their team. You can discuss as a class what's good about each of the sentences and how they could be further improved.

You can repeat these steps several times with different sentences. A timer on the board should help with the pace and prevent students from going off-task.

First letter

'This is my go-to exercise when I need a nice quick-prep starter activity.'

This could be used as a starter activity to see how much students have remembered from the previous lesson or it could even be used to check student progress within a lesson.

Provide students with the first letter of each word in a sentence you have created. These could simply be displayed on the whiteboard to save paper. The students then try to guess what word each letter represents.

For example, on the topic of food the sentence could be:

A pd j m d c a d l = **A**u **p**etit-**d**éjeuner **j**e **m**ange **d**es **c**éréales **a**vec **d**u **l**ait.

Some students may also come up with alternative but accurate sentences that you hadn't even considered yourself. If students are struggling, they could be given the English translation or they could look through the notes in their book from the previous lesson to help them.

You can then ask your students to translate these sentences into English. As an extra challenge, they could try to further develop each sentence – for example by justifying an opinion, adding another tense or including the third person.

Teaching tip

Provide your students with picture clues to help them figure out each sentence.

Taking it further

Ask students to come up with several sentences for homework and make a note of the first letter for each of the words. The starter activity next lesson could be to swap with their partner and guess each other's sentences.

Structure strips

'By giving students the sentence starters during a written exercise, it helps to keep them focused and prevents them from going off on a tangent.'

Some students find it really hard to get stuck in when they are asked to produce a piece of writing. They know their destination, but they are not quite sure how to get there. Structure strips are a way of guiding your students and ensuring that they include all the key elements for a successful piece of writing.

When I first started teaching, I remember asking a class to produce a piece of writing about themselves. This should have been a straightforward task. We had practised the vocabulary and I was confident that they knew it well. They had a checklist of what features to include in a piece of writing to make it successful. Cue 30 confused faces and a lot of pen tapping. This wasn't enough and they clearly needed more guidance. I was delighted when I stumbled across Stephen Lockyer's (@mrlockyer) 'structure strips'. He created this technique for helping his primary students structure their written work. I've seen this used by many secondary teachers too and it has revolutionised my teaching.

Structure strips are sheets resembling bookmarks that can be stuck in the margin of a sheet of paper or the student's exercise book. They include several boxes containing information on what to include in each of their paragraphs to help students to structure their work. Each box could contain sentence starters, as well as a checklist of what to include in each paragraph. This really helps to focus the students and they can even tick each feature they have included as they go along.

Advanced students can be challenged by adding an extension to each of the boxes, for example: 'Say what you were like when you were younger' – 'Quand j'étais plus jeune... ', or 'Say where you would like to live' – 'Dans le futur je voudrais habiter... '.

For less able students, you could include tips and reminders of other resources they could refer to, to help them. For example: 'For more information on the conditional, look at the independent learning folder.' (This is in Idea 47.)

You will probably need to 'wean' your students off structure strips at some point, as obviously they won't be permitted in any exams and you will want them to be fully prepared for this. However, after using them a few times you could set students the task of asking them to produce their own structure strips as part of their planning.

Examples of Spanish structure strips can be found in the online resources.

IDEA 41

Perfect paragraphs

'Students enjoyed reading, peer-assessing and improving each other's work.'

This activity can be used to support students prior to them producing their own individual written piece.

Teaching tip

Firstly, do this exercise as a class using the visualiser method (see Idea 91), before allowing students to work in groups. This could be using an example you have prepared or another student's work (with their permission, of course).

Students work in groups to produce a short piece of writing on a particular topic. Allow a set amount of time for this. Again, a timer on the board should help with the pace. At the end of the allocated time, students move to a different table and try to improve another group's paragraph. This could be done several times, so that they are peer-assessing several groups' work.

As with any peer-assessment activity, students will probably need a fair bit of guidance with this, such as a checklist of things to look for and improve:

- Are spellings accurate?
- Are capital letters and punctuation used appropriately?
- Is there a range of adjectives?
- Have they avoided repetition where possible?
- Have they used a variety of tenses?
- Have they included opinions? Are the opinions justified?
- Have they included complex sentences?
- Have they included a range of connectives?
- Have they included quantifiers?

Students can discuss at the end what changes were made and why, and what they liked about each paragraph. This is a good way of reminding students what they need to include in a successful written piece, and should also highlight any common errors. You can then discuss these with your class, and it should help them with their accuracy when producing their own writing.

Bonus idea ★

It may also be useful to give each group a different-coloured pen so you can see where changes were made and by whom.

Phrase of the week

'This is a way to motivate students to experiment with new language in their written work.'

Students aim to produce higher-quality written work by including the phrase of the week and are then rewarded for their efforts.

For this idea, you simply need to display a 'phrase of the week' in the target language on the board or somewhere in your classroom, along with its English translation. If you teach more than one language, these could be displayed on the board next to the flag of the country where that language is spoken. You could use the same phrase of the week for all classes and year groups, or have a few different ones, depending on your students' ability or relating to the topics that they are studying.

The phrases should be ones your students haven't encountered previously, such as idioms or verb phrases – the types of phrases that could perhaps earn them a few extra marks in a written exam.

Make your students aware that they have the opportunity to earn rewards for using these phrases in their written work, providing that they are used accurately and in context. Personally, I like to give out raffle tickets to each student who has used it correctly. I draw out a ticket each week and that student wins a prize.

Teaching tip

Come up with a list of phrases as a department and plan which one will be used each week. This consistency and repetition of seeing the same phrase will be useful for shared classes.

Colourful sentences

'A simple but effective way of helping students to create sentences.'

Here is a way of supporting students with their written work and helping them with their word order.

Teaching tip

A Spanish template for this activity can be found in the online resources.

Students are given different-coloured cards with individual words or phrases on them relating to the topic you are currently teaching. They then work in pairs putting the cards together to produce sentences, having been told the order in which the colours should go. As an extra challenge, see whether students can figure out the order the colours should go in themselves.

For example, when teaching subordinating conjunctions and hobbies in German, students could be given cards with the vocabulary below and asked to form sentences. All opinion phrases will be on one colour of card, and so on. This activity should help them to remember that some connectives send the verb to the end of the sentence.

Opinion phrase	Hobby	Connective	Pronoun	Adjective	Verb
Ich liebe	Fußball spielen,	weil	es	aktiv	ist.
Ich mag	schwimmen,	wenn	es	sonnig	ist.
Ich mag	lesen,	weil	es	entspannend	ist.
Ich hasse	Sport machen,	obwohl	es	wichtig	ist.

Taking it further

Students could further develop each sentence where appropriate.

Again, this is easily adaptable for different languages, topics and abilities. The number of cards given would depend on the ability of the group. With less able groups, focus on just a few sentences and do not give too many cards, so as not to overwhelm your students.

Sharing successes

'Students are more keen to take pride in the presentation of their work, if it can be photographed and emailed home to their parents.'

This is one way to encourage students to give you their best work and to be rewarded for it.

One of my bugbears when it comes to marking students' work is when I can see that they have made little effort when it comes to the presentation. Taking pride in their work is important and shouldn't be overlooked, especially as they will most likely need to use these notes to revise from later on.

Mo Ladak (@MathedUp) shared his 'request a selfie' idea, in which he invites his students to draw a camera next to any work they have produced that they are particularly proud of. The teacher then takes a photo of this work and sends it home to parents.

In my classroom I have a sign that reads 'Proud of your work?' with some pegs clipped to it. Each peg has a clip art image of a camera glued to it. If students are really proud of their work and want to show it off, they are encouraged to help themselves to a peg and attach it to that particular piece of work. When I mark their books, if I'm also happy with the presentation and think it deserves recognition, I can then take a photo and quickly send this home to parents via email, or share this on our departmental Twitter page for fellow students and parents to see.

This is a quick and easy way to keep parents informed without taking up too much of your time. It's a great way to celebrate successes and the students always appreciate teachers taking the time to send a quick positive email home.

> **Taking it further**
>
> Set up an MFL department blog where you can keep parents informed of topics being covered each term and showcase students' best work.

Dice gap fill

'This works really well with reluctant writers.'

This is a great kinaesthetic idea that works well with less able students to support them in producing their own written piece.

Taking it further

For those students who finish quickly, give them an example in English to be translated into the target language, using the vocabulary on the sheet to help them.

Provide students with a text with certain words missing from each sentence, as well as a grid with six possible answers for each of the gaps. The aim is for students to produce an example piece of writing, which they can use later as a model for writing their own version.

Here is a shortened version of an example text, followed by an example answer grid:

Je m'appelle Marc et j'ai (a) _____ ans. J'habite avec (b) _____ dans une petite maison en Angleterre. Dans le futur je voudrais habiter dans (c) _____ aux États-Unis.

	a	b	c
1	huit	ma famille	une grande maison
2	neuf	mes parents	une ferme
3	dix	mes grands-parents	un appartement
4	onze	ma sœur	un château
5	douze	mon copain	une maison de plain-pied
6	treize	ma mère	un chalet

Students can work individually rolling the dice, finding the corresponding words in the grid and then filling the gaps. For example, if a student rolls 1 – 3 – 5, their text would say:

Je m'appelle Marc et j'ai (a) **huit** ans. J'habite avec (b) **mes grands-parents** dans une petite maison en Angleterre. Dans le futur je voudrais habiter dans (c) **une maison de plain-pied** aux États-Unis.

Some students may be able to produce several different versions in the time you allow. They can then swap texts with their partner and translate each other's into English.

Photocard preparation

'This starter activity, if done regularly enough, is a good way to develop students' confidence at tackling the photocard element of the speaking exam by writing down their descriptions.'

This starter activity helps get students used to describing what they can see.

At the start of a lesson, provide each student with a different image relating to the current topic, e.g. if you are currently studying the topic of 'home and local area', each student could be given a different picture of a bedroom. Put a timer on the board and give students a few minutes to write a description of the picture the best they can in the target language.

This activity can easily be tailored to suit your students' abilities. With an able group, you could challenge them by asking them to describe the photo using vocabulary from their memory. With a less able group, you may wish to display some sentence starters and key vocabulary on the board as extra support, or you could give them the description in English to be translated into the target language.

This could then lead into a speaking and listening activity. Choose several students to read out their descriptions, while the others listen carefully and, on mini whiteboards, produce a rough drawing of what they think the bedroom looks like.

Alternatively, several photos could be displayed on the board to save on printing costs and students decide which one they want to describe. This can also be used as a listening activity, as they can read out their descriptions while their classmates try to figure out which of the images on the board they have chosen.

Teaching tip

Keep a box of laminated photo cards relating to different topics. These can be used again and again with different classes.

Grammar

Part 5

Independent learning folders

'Miss, how do you say, "This weekend I'm going to the cinema"?'

The independent learning folders are one of my favourite classroom resources for promoting student independence. I have produced them in both French and Spanish, but they could easily be adapted for other languages.

Teaching tip

These could be uploaded to the virtual learning environment (VLE) for students to access at home. Make parents and carers aware of this at parents' evening, so that they can encourage their children to practise at home.

I created these resources quite early on in my teaching career, when I found that students, when producing written work, would ask me how to say phrases that used tenses we hadn't covered yet in class. This left me with several options. I could sit down with the student and explain the tense to them, which of course takes time and would prevent me from circulating the room and helping other students. Alternatively, I could simply ask them to leave this out of their work for now, which would be holding them back. Or I could simply tell them the translation, which meant that students would start to view me as a walking dictionary and ask me for translations for everything.

I created the independent learning folders (suggestions for a catchier title welcome!) to enable my students to become more independent, and they are now one of my most-used resources.

The folders include guides on a variety of tenses:

- present tense
- imperfect tense
- perfect tense/preterite tense
- conditional tense
- future tense
- near future tense.

Each page gives examples of the tense in both English and the target language. This helps because students are often unsure of which tense they need to use. It also includes straightforward, step-by-step instructions on how to form the tense, some time and frequency phrases that can be used alongside each tense and a QR code that links to further support (e.g. websites, quizzes/games to allow them to practise the tense) if needed.

There are also pages on:

- time and frequency phrases
- giving extra detail
- giving opinions.

In my classroom, I have found it useful to have five folders (one per desk) that contain each sheet printed out and laminated. These can be kept on desks or somewhere in the classroom where students can easily find them, so that they can access them whenever they need to. Remember, the aim is to promote independence.

These folders are great for mixed-ability groups, as it gives the more able students opportunities to challenge themselves by discovering and using new tenses not yet taught. The student-friendly, easy-to-read format allows less able students to easily catch up if they are struggling.

Bonus idea ★

Students could also use these when acting on feedback in the teacher's marking, to help them to improve their work. For example, if a student has been instructed to check their present tense verb endings, they can quickly and easily find this information in the folder if they need to.

Mini whiteboard tenses

'Ask any teacher what their most useful classroom resource is and I'm sure most of them would say mini whiteboards!'

This activity works best if you have a full class set of mini whiteboards and pens. I have used this particular exercise when practising new tenses with both Key Stage 3 and Key Stage 4, as it is easily adaptable for any ability.

Teaching tip

This activity would work well following the 'Flippin' grammar' idea (see Idea 56).

After teaching the rules for forming the tense in question, provide students with a whiteboard and pen each. Give students an infinitive in the target language to write down on their boards. Then give them a verb phrase in English that they have to conjugate. I find it helps to keep it reasonably simple by starting with regular verbs of the same ending, e.g. regular 'er' verbs in French.

Firstly, ask the students what the steps of forming the tense are. If they've been paying attention and have understood the tense formation rules, they'll know to simply rub off the infinitive ending so that they are just left with the stem. They'll know to add the correct pronoun at the beginning and the correct verb ending that goes with it.

Once you have checked all their answers and are happy they have understood, give them another verb phrase to translate, this time simply changing the pronoun. Students keep the stem already written on their boards, but will need to change the pronoun and the verb ending. The next time you can use the same pronoun but choose a different infinitive, so the ending and pronoun stay the same and only the stem changes.

I find it useful to ask different students to talk through the process each time. This repetition and practice will really help some of the students who were perhaps just not getting it before.

Chocolate bar infinitives

'Chocolate is a great way of motivating my students.'

Sadly, not all students share my love of grammar. This is a way to make tense revision a bit more enjoyable.

This idea, which was shared by Jennifer Beattie (@nowMrsMFL), can be used when teaching any tense in any language. After you have practised a new tense, this is a good way of testing how well the students have retained what you taught them.

Buy some chocolate bars and put a sticky label on each one, with a different infinitive written on it in the target language. You will need to buy chocolate bars that have six pieces. Each piece of the bar represents one of the six parts of a verb.

There are two ways to run the activity. In the first, you use a random name generator to select a student. This student then has the opportunity to conjugate all six parts of the verb written on the chocolate bar in the tense you have been practising. They could do this verbally or write them up on the whiteboard. For each part they conjugate accurately, they earn a piece of that chocolate bar.

Alternatively, this could be done as a whole-class activity to ensure greater participation. Give each student a mini whiteboard and pen and ask them to conjugate all six parts of the verb, writing on their boards and covering up their answers. Then you can randomly select a student to share their answers. For each one they have written correctly, they earn a piece of the chocolate bar. If they get any wrong, give another student the chance to earn the other parts of the chocolate bar.

Taking it further

Students could continue to work on their tenses independently using Dr Gianfranco Conti's 'The Language Gym' (www.language-gym.com).

Five-minute tense challenge

'Things may get a little tense (ba-dum ching) in this starter activity...'

Students work against the clock to conjugate five infinitives in a given tense in just five minutes.

Teaching tip

You could use Classtools for the timer (www. classtools.net/timer).

Taking it further

Students could then translate the verbs into English or produce sentences using a verb from each column.

This exercise works really well once the rules of forming a particular tense have been established. If done regularly, this method of tense revision is invaluable for instilling confidence. As well as practising tenses covered recently, it is useful for revising tenses learnt last term or even last year.

Firstly, provide students with a grid similar to the German example below (see the online resources for a printable version). Introduce the task, and put a five-minute timer on the board to ensure the pace and encourage students to focus better.

Conjugate the infinitives below in the present tense. You have five minutes. *irregular					
	spielen	**wohnen**	**kochen**	**schwimmen**	**essen***
ich					
du					
er/sie/es					
wir					
ihr					
sie					

Depending on the ability of the group, you may wish to give a combination of regular and irregular verbs, or fewer infinitives. Encourage students to do this activity from memory; however, if they are really struggling, they could use the independent learning folders (see Idea 47), their own notes or the grammar section in the textbook. After the five minutes are up, it is helpful to ask students to explain the verb formation rules for that particular tense.

Roll a verb

'This is a really useful activity when consolidating tenses.'

A grammar activity in which students roll the dice and conjugate the corresponding infinitive.

Before the lesson, prepare some 7 x 7 blank verb grids similar to the one below, including just the infinitives and pronouns. A printable version can be downloaded from the online resources.

	1 spielen	2 fragen	3 sagen	4 machen	5 laufen	6 fahren
1 ich						
2 du						
3 er/sie/es						
4 wir						
5 ihr						
6 sie						

Give each student a printed grid and a dice. Alternatively, they could share and work in pairs. Students roll the dice twice, then fill in the correct box on the grid, conjugating one of the six infinitives for one of the six pronouns in the tense you want them to practise. For example, if a student rolls a two and a three, they must conjugate *fragen* in the third person singular.

It may be useful to provide students with the rules for conjugating the chosen tense and remind them of key things they may need to look out for, e.g. does the verb take *haben* or *sein*? Allow students a set amount of time to complete this, and you may wish to display a timer on the board to help keep the pace.

Teaching tip

If students are finding it difficult to conjugate verbs in a particular tense, apps such as Verb Blitz are available to help them practise this independently.

Bonus idea ★

Provide students with a filled-in grid and this exercise could be done as a translation activity instead, with students translating the verb phrases from the target language into English.

Verb swap shop

'Practice makes perfect.'

This is an excellent way to consolidate students' knowledge and understanding of a particular tense and requires little preparation from the teacher.

I normally allow students to work in pairs for this activity, but individually or in groups would work fine too. Every pair is given a sheet of paper with a picture of a flower with six petals on it. A template can be downloaded from the online resources. Each sheet should have a different infinitive in the target language written in the middle of the flower.

In pairs, they discuss how to conjugate that verb in the first person singular in the tense chosen by you, and then write this in one of the petals. They pass the sheet on and conjugate the next infinitive for the second person singular in the next petal, and so on and so forth until they have conjugated six different infinitives and each petal is filled in.

I have found that the repetition in this activity is good for training students on how verbs are formed, spotting patterns and recognising the similarities and differences between verbs. With a less able group, you may want to stick to similar infinitives, such as using all regular 'ar' verbs for Spanish, so that they only have to remember one set of endings in the beginning. With more advanced students, it is a good idea to challenge them by using a range of verbs, e.g. regular and irregular verbs, and verbs with different endings.

One pen, one dice

'This makes practising tenses a bit more fun, Miss.'

This is one of my favourite activities for motivating students and is great for keeping them focused when doing grammar work.

I've seen several variations of this game, but I generally use this when practising tenses. Students work in pairs. Each student has a sheet of verbs to conjugate in the tense chosen by the teacher. This could be a tense that you are currently teaching or perhaps a tense that the students have learnt previously but need to revise. The aim of the game is to be the first in your pair to complete the sheet.

The catch? There is only one pen per pair. One student starts holding the pen and working through the sheet, correctly answering as many questions as possible. Their partner has the dice and keeps rolling it until they roll a six and can take the pen from the other student. They can then work through the sheet while their partner rolls the dice, until a six is rolled again and they can take the pen back.

The student who is the first to accurately complete all conjugations is the winner. Answers could be quickly checked as a class, or students could be provided with an answer sheet so that they can check their own.

An example worksheet for this activity can be found in the online resources.

Teaching tip

Give each student a different sheet to prevent them from copying their partner's answers.

Taking it further

Students could be asked to conjugate the verbs in a range of tenses, instead of just focusing on one.

Bonus idea ★

This activity can be adapted by giving students a sheet of words, phrases or sentences to translate instead of conjugating verbs.

YouTube videos

'Videos are one way to capture your students' interest.'

When I think back to my own school days, I remember feeling so excited about the prospect of watching a video in class. However, gone are the days of the teacher having to wheel a TV into the classroom. Nowadays, most of us are fortunate to have computer access in our classrooms and, with a few clicks of a button, we can have millions of videos at our fingertips. Many of these are suitable for supporting our MFL teaching.

Tutorials and songs that explain various grammar points can make a nice change from teacher talk and PowerPoints. Students could watch these, make notes and feed back to you at the end. I've lost count of the amount of times I've used the 'Agree It' YouTube video to explain adjectival agreements in Spanish – it's silly, but it's engaging and memorable (www.youtube.com/watch?v=80O0q9e-mHQ).

Clips of children's TV programmes such as *Peppa Pig* and *Thomas and Friends*, as well as popular series such as *Friends*, are available in a range of languages. Students could watch one of these, write down any examples of verbs in a particular tense, then translate these into English afterwards. This also doubles up as a listening activity, by providing students with the transcript with words missing and asking them to fill in the gaps while watching the clip. Alternatively, provide students with a transcript of the video containing errors, and students have to highlight and correct the errors.

All of these activities could be done in class or as a homework task by providing students with the gap-fill sheet and link to take home with them. You may wish to include a QR code that students can scan, enabling them to access the link more easily.

Bonus idea ★

Students could create their own videos on a particular topic for homework. Show these to the class next lesson and vote on the winners, who could win a prize.

Battleships

'This is a fun way to practise conjugating verbs in a particular tense.'

A classic game that can be easily adapted for use as an MFL speaking exercise to practise tenses.

Prepare a 7 x 7 grid with pronouns down the side and infinitives along the top (in English or the target language), then print these off with two grids to a page. This grid could be used for regular present tense 'er' verbs in French.

	play	talk	sing	dance	listen	draw
I						
You singular		x				
He/she						
We			x	x		
You plural						
They		x	x	x		

Students plot their ships on their own grid. They mark an X in one box (the submarine), in a line of two boxes (the battleship) and in a line of three boxes (the carrier). They then take turns trying to guess where the other player's ships are by calling out plot points, saying the pronoun and the verb correctly (e.g. 'je joue'). On their second grid, students mark their shots with X if they hit one of their opponent's ships or O if they miss, according to the opposing player's response. If the other player hits one of your battleships, put a line through the box on your own grid. All boxes in the line must be hit in order to sink the ship.

For example, if the opposing player says 'tu parles', they have sunk my submarine. If they say 'nous chantons', they have hit my battleship. If they then say 'nous dansons', they have sunk my battleship. The first player to sink all of the enemy's ships is the winner.

Teaching tip

If you feel some students may struggle to remember the verb endings, you could allow them access to the independent learning folders (Idea 47) as support.

Bonus idea ★

This activity could also be used for practising time phrases and hobbies. Write time phrases down the side of the grid and hobbies along the top in English.

Flippin' grammar

'Learn it at home. Master it in school.'

This flipped learning technique allows us to really make the most of what little time we have with our students as MFL teachers.

Flipped learning is where students are given the content prior to a lesson, so that class time is used to explore these concepts in more depth and spend more time practising them.

Firstly, students are given information to look through at home. This could be information on a particular tense or another grammatical feature, such as adjective agreements. It should include an explanation with examples. Students read through the information in their own time before the next lesson and make notes in their books, writing about what they have learned in their own words. Instruct them to write down any questions they may have for you. They could then be given a quiz to complete at home to practise what they have learned.

Websites such as Kahoot (see Idea 78 for more information) and Sporcle are a great way of doing this and have plenty of ready-made quizzes on a variety of topics. They are interactive, meaning that students get instant feedback and they do all the marking for you, so you don't have to. Win–win! It is important that students are doing something active with the information given to them. They are more likely to have a greater understanding of the concept if they have practised applying it, rather than simply read about it.

The next lesson, invite your students to work in pairs, sharing what they have learned and what they found challenging, while you circulate the room. They can then talk in groups, before discussing it as a class and asking any questions they prepared at home. This is a good way to gauge how much of the content was understood correctly and allows you to address any misconceptions. Once you are happy that the students have a good understanding of the content, they then have the rest of the lesson to spend time mastering it and developing their confidence through a range of activities chosen by you.

You could use one or a combination of the following examples of home learning resources:

- The sheets from my **independent learning folders** (available in the accompanying online resources in French and Spanish, but can be adapted for other languages – more information in Idea 47). They could either be printed off and given to students or uploaded to the school's VLE to save on printing costs.
- **YouTube videos** – there are many already made or you could make your own. If you are using one of the ready-made videos, I suggest that you watch it carefully first to make sure that it is suitable for your students.
- Useful websites such as **BBC Bitesize.**
- **Slideshare** – upload a PowerPoint tutorial and easily share this with students.
- **Powtoon** – a website that allows you to create engaging videos and presentations that can be easily shared with students, or students could even create their own!

Taking it further

After the lesson, students could then produce their own Powtoon presentation, demonstrating their learning.

Verb towers

'A game that can be played when practising any tense.'

Students work in small groups, taking it in turns to conjugate verbs, earn bricks and compete against each other to build the tallest tower.

Taking it further

With a more able class, you can make this activity even more challenging by adding a second set of cards, each one with a tense written on it. In this variation of the game, students would have to conjugate verbs in a range of tenses instead of just the one.

For this exercise, you will need some packs of wooden blocks (one pack per team), with each block colour-coded to match one of the six pronouns. Lego blocks in six different colours would also work with this activity. You will also need to prepare a pack of cards, each one with an infinitive written on it – either regular or a mixture of regular and irregular if you want to add an extra challenge. You may wish to print irregular verbs on different-coloured card to make it easier for students to distinguish between them.

Students sit around a table with a pile of wooden blocks and a pile of cards in the middle. They take it in turns to choose, at random, a wooden block and a card. They then say the conjugation of their verb for that pronoun out loud to the other players in their group, while the others listen carefully and decide whether the answer is correct. Allow them access to their notes or the independent learning folders (see Idea 47) when checking each other's answers.

If the player is correct, they are allowed to keep their block. If they answer incorrectly, they must return the block to the pile. Each time they answer correctly, they can keep their block and add to their tower. If their tower collapses before the end of the game, they must start again. By the end of the game, the player with the tallest tower is the winner.

Translation

Part 6

Mini whiteboard translations

'Less able students seem more comfortable using mini whiteboards and are more likely to attempt an answer, whereas they may be reluctant to do so in their exercise books for fear of having a permanent record of any errors.'

Mini whiteboards can be one of the best learning tools for translation work. They allow for greater student participation and show instantly how much students have understood.

Teaching tip

Don't hand out the pens until you've explained the task. This will hopefully ensure that you have students' full attention during the explanation and prevent them from wasting time doodling.

Lessons can be dominated by more confident and enthusiastic students, who may find it hard not to shout out an answer. More introverted students may be reluctant to even raise their hand to answer a question, and dread speaking in front of the class, afraid of making a mistake. This translation activity encourages whole-class participation and allows you to monitor the progress of all students without bringing the quieter students *too far* out of their comfort zones.

Simply read out a phrase in English and give students a limited amount of time to write out the translation on their mini whiteboards. Restricting the amount of time students have to write their answers should help with pace and limit opportunities to go off task. You can then go through the answers with the class. It may be useful to have the correct answers ready on a PowerPoint, to enable students to quickly mark their own work. I ask students to check each word carefully and tick every correct one.

If all students' answers are correct, you can move on to the next translation. If some are incorrect, this shows that you will need to dedicate more time to re-teaching and addressing any misunderstandings. I remind my students that mistakes are valuable learning opportunities and other students in the class will also benefit from this.

Pass the parcel

'How can I keep my students interested towards the end of the lesson?'

Use this engaging plenary to practise the translation of key phrases you have covered in the lesson.

Prepare some cards with sentences on them using familiar language – a combination of both English and target language works well. You could wrap these up as for the pass the parcel game of childhood birthday parties, or just put them in a box.

At the end of the lesson, students pass the parcel around the room, while you play music in the target language. You could display the song lyrics on the board so that students can sing along and practise the pronunciation while they wait for the box to be passed to them. When you stop the music, the student holding the parcel takes out a sentence and translates it.

You could also put some sweets in the box to motivate students, who take one if they translate correctly. Rebecca Owen (@owen_ becca) shared her *I'm a Celebrity Get Me Out of Here*-themed activity, where she hid questions in a green box filled with strawberry laces and jelly snakes.

Differentiate this activity according to the needs of your students. You could colour-code the cards (green – foundation, orange – intermediate, red – higher) and encourage your students to choose one that appropriately challenges them. Alternatively, keep all cards the same colour but with each one containing a sentence to translate, as well as an optional extra challenge for students to complete, such as changing the tense, making the sentence negative, or adapting/extending the sentence.

Teaching tip

Instead of sentences to translate, you could prepare grammar questions relating to one or several tenses and students could try to answer these.

Translation grids

'How can I make sure students don't miss out words in translation exercises?'

This method of helping students to structure their answers ensures that they translate the sentences in full.

For some translations, such as sentences including French and Spanish adjectives, or subordinating conjunctions in German, remind students to carefully consider the word order beforehand.

Students are given a sheet of sentences to translate into the target language, based on what they have been learning recently in class. Each word of the translation has its own individual box in a grid for students to write in. By providing students with the first letter of each word, this encourages them to focus on each individual word in the sentence and it means that they are less likely to miss out certain words. For example: Last year I went on holiday to Paris with my friends.

Grid given to students:

L'a	d	j	s	a
e	v	à	P	a
m	a .			

Provide students with a QR code with a link to the answers to allow them to self-assess.

Grid when completed:

L'année	dernière	je	suis	allé
en	vacances	à	Paris	avec
mes	amis.			

You may wish to give your students more or fewer letters, depending on their ability. For example, more able students may not have a letter in every box, whereas less able students may require the first three letters of each word. Complete examples can be found in the online resources.

Be a smartie

'Anything chocolate-related has to go down well, surely?'

For this exercise, you will need a tube of Smarties® and (if you are anything like me) a whole lot of willpower not to eat them all yourself before the lesson.

Thank you to the wonderful Laura Scott (@mrsscottmfl), who adapted the 'Be a smartie' idea for MFL as a way of motivating students. This works really well as a plenary to check their understanding, but could also be used as a retrieval practice starter activity.

Once you have finished teaching and practising the new content with your class, allow your students to each pick a Smartie® from the tube. Display eight different-coloured sentences on the board – these can be in English or the target language or even a mixture of the two. Students then write down the translation of the sentence that matches the colour of their Smartie®. When they translate it correctly (quickly checked by yourself in the lesson), they can eat their Smartie®.

Alternatively, instead of sentences to translate, there could be eight different tasks to complete.

Here are some examples:

- Name six words/phrases you learnt today.
- Extend this sentence.
- Add an opinion to this sentence.
- Make this sentence negative.
- Change the tense in this sentence.
- Put these words in the correct order to create an accurate sentence.

Bonus idea ★

For a great revision activity to practise speaking skills, put students into groups, giving each group a pack of Smarties®. They take it in turns to pick out a Smartie®, each colour representing a different topic that they have to discuss in their groups.

IDEA 62

Get them Pinterested

'If you haven't yet discovered Pinterest, you've been missing out.'

This is a nice starter activity, used as a translation exercise, or as a way of introducing students to a new topic.

Teaching tip

Create a Pinterest board of these images and provide your students with the link and QR code for the board as a way to promote language learning outside of the classroom. A separate board for each language is a good idea or you may confuse your students.

Bonus idea

You can also use Pinterest to create a teaching board to help with your lesson planning. It is so easy to find inspiration when you are lacking ideas for your lessons and you could easily share this board with your colleagues.

Pinterest (www.pinterest.com) allows users to upload images or add their own from another website. You can then create different boards and either add your own images to these or re-pin those uploaded by other people. These can be private or public and you also have the option of inviting other people to pin things to your board. I have used Pinterest for a range of things, from finding inspiration for my wedding to looking for exciting new recipes. However, as I am about to explain, you can also use this site as a teaching aid.

A quick Pinterest search will come up with hundreds and hundreds of internet memes, cartoons and quotes on a variety of topics in a range of languages – simply type your topic and language into the search bar. There are lots of images relating to the topic of technology, for example. Then print these off for a quick-prep starter activity. Laminate them and you will be able to use them over and over again with different classes. Hand these out to students or leave them on desks at the start of the lesson and simply ask students to translate them into English or to consider what topic they are about to begin.

Dartboard translations

'A jazzed-up translation exercise.'

Students work in small teams competing against their peers to earn the most points in this translation plenary activity.

Divide the class into teams of three or four. Then say sentences in English, which the students have to translate into the target language. Ask each team to work together to come up with an accurate translation, and then write this down on their mini whiteboards or in their books. If they are struggling to come up with an answer, you may wish to allow them to refer back to any notes they have.

Give them a time limit to come up with their answers and then ask them to hold up their boards to allow you to quickly check their answers. Any group who has the answer written correctly can earn 50 points. You could award fewer points to any teams who almost have the answer but aren't quite there.

For the first round, if Team 1 have the answer correct, they have an opportunity to score some bonus points for their team by throwing a dart at the dartboard. If they manage to get their dart on the board, the number they hit is the amount of extra points they win. This also allows for an opportunity to practise numbers in the target language. Repeat the above steps and allow Team 2 an opportunity to earn bonus points, and so on and so forth.

> **Teaching tip**
>
> Visit your local pound shop and buy one of the cheap dartboards. I recommend the velcro ones to avoid any nasty accidents.

Mosaic writing

'This really gets my students thinking carefully about sentence structure and choosing the best translation.'

Dr Gianfranco Conti shares lots of incredible ideas, both in his book *(The Language Teacher Toolkit)*, which he co-authored alongside Steve Smith (@spsmith45), and online via social media (@gianfrancocont9) and on his website (https://gianfrancoconti. wordpress.com). One of my favourites is his 'Mosaic writing' idea, which is easily adaptable for a range of abilities.

Teaching tip

It is a good idea to work through the first one together as a class, before asking students to work through the sheet independently.

Prepare a grid of phrases in the target language and several numbered sentences in English underneath. Each column should contain one part of one of the sentences below the grid; however, the sentences should be jumbled up on different rows. Students should aim to find the best translation of their English sentence and then write the number in one of the boxes in each column of the grid. Alternatively, students could colour each sentence in a different colour.

Here is a shortened example:

Quand j'ai le temps	je préfère 1	écouter de la musique	avec 1	mes copains. 1
Normalement 1	j'aime	faire du shopping	avec	ma chambre.
Quelquefois	j'adore	regarder la télé 1	dans	ma mère.

Bonus idea ★

Leave one English sentence out. Students can then translate the sentence left in the grid into English.

1 Normally I prefer to watch TV with my friends.
2 Sometimes I like to go shopping with my mum.
3 When I have the time I love to listen to music in my bedroom.

Anticipate any parts of the translation that could cause confusion and provide students with a support sheet of reminders for these, e.g. In French they say 'to do shopping' instead of 'to go shopping'.

Smith, S. and Conti, G. (2016), *The Language Teacher Toolkit*. California, US: CreateSpace Independent Publishing.

Translation four in a row

'My students loved playing this adaptation of the Connect 4® game.'

This two-player game is a hands-on, fun way to practise and develop students' translation skills.

Before the lesson, create a 6 x 7 grid of 42 boxes. Each of the boxes should have a phrase written in it, either in English or in the target language. This could be vocabulary that you have covered recently in class or it can be done as a revision exercise, by choosing vocabulary from topics you have looked at throughout the year. You may find it useful to print out another copy with the translations, so that students can easily check their answers if they are unsure.

Put the students in pairs and give them one grid between two, but make sure that they have a different-coloured highlighter pen each. Students take it in turns to translate one of the phrases on the grid. The other player has to decide whether the answer is correct or not. If they manage to answer correctly, they can highlight that phrase using their pen. The turn then passes to the other player.

The aim of the game is to highlight four phrases in a row – this could be horizontally, vertically or diagonally.

Bonus idea ★

This game could also be adapted and used as a way of preparing students for the photocard element of the exams. Put an image in each of the boxes and the students have to come up with a sentence to describe it. If they can come up with an accurate sentence, they can highlight the image. The first to highlight four images in a row is the winner.

Tangled translations

'The best translation activity I've ever done!'

This translation activity is suitable for a range of abilities, but has worked particularly well with less able students, who find it less daunting due to half of the words already being translated.

Before the lesson, you will need to prepare a 'Tangled translation' sheet to be given to your students. At the top of the page include a paragraph on the topic you are currently working on and containing vocabulary your students should be mostly familiar with. Half of the words in the text should be in English, and the other half should be written in the target language, with the word order following that of the target language. Underneath the paragraph add two empty boxes – one will eventually be filled in by the students with the complete English version and the other box with the complete target language version.

Firstly, give your students a sheet each, and then ask them to highlight the words in two different colours, depending on whether they are in English or in the target language. Alternatively, you could give this to them with the target language parts in bold. Students then write out the English translation in full and the target language translation in full in the boxes below the text.

Here is a short example:

I live à Southampton en Angleterre in a small maison modern with mon dad et my sœur.	
English	**Français**
I live in Southampton in England in a small modern house with my dad and my sister.	J'habite à Southampton en Angleterre dans une petite maison moderne avec mon père et ma sœur.

Cryptic translations

'A challenging starter that students always enjoy!'

This is an activity that encourages dictionary use. It allows the students to have fun while developing their dictionary and translation skills.

For this exercise, students can work individually or in teams. They are given cryptic clues for celebrities' names, which they have to translate into English using dictionaries or WordReference (www.wordreference.com) to help them. These clues can be displayed on the board as a starter activity for students to complete when they enter the classroom.

Here are some examples of cryptic clues I have used in the past with my students:

1 británico rodilla lanzas – Britney Spears
2 justo en madera lago – Justin Timberlake
3 sastre rápido – Taylor Swift
4 arrendajo me zorro – Jamie Foxx
5 poder sí oeste – Kanye West

This exercise is a good way to show the students that sometimes words will have several translations in English and they have to find the one that best fits and makes the most sense. When looking at the above examples, *rápido* means 'quick' in Spanish. However, a synonym for 'quick' in English is 'swift'. *Justo* can mean 'fair' or 'just' and *madera* can mean 'wood' or 'timber'.

Taking it further

If some of the students finish the exercise quickly, ask them to create some of their own cryptic clues in the target language to share with the class at the end.

Bonus idea ★

Another great starter idea that students love to do is translating song and film titles or TV programmes into English.

Noughts and crosses translations

'Noughts and crosses translation is a minimal-prep game that allows me to consolidate what my students have learned during the lesson.'

This MFL twist on the classic game works well as a plenary, helping pupils to reflect on what they have learned throughout the lesson.

This game could work in either of the following ways:

Idea 1: Draw a 3 x 3 grid up on the board, with each box of the grid containing a phrase in English relating to the current topic.

Idea 2: If you are more technologically minded, prepare a PowerPoint slide with a 3 x 3 grid prior to the lesson. Each box of the grid could contain an image or a phrase in English relating to the current topic. There should be some noughts and crosses next to the grid, which can be easily clicked and dragged when the game is being played.

Split the class into two groups – the 'noughts' and the 'crosses'. Next, ask them to take it in turns to either come up with a sentence in the target language for the images on the board or translate the English phrases into the target language. If they answer correctly, they can either draw or drag their nought or cross into that box in the grid. The first group to line up three in a row are the winners.

Vocabulary

Part 7

Five a day MFL

'But I knew all the words yesterday when I learnt them, Miss!'

Ahead of vocabulary tests, students are often given a list of words to take away and learn at home. From experience, students can feel that just staring at the words is sufficient to memorise them, but then they struggle to recall the spellings when it comes to sitting the actual test. Sometimes students just don't know how to revise the vocabulary.

This idea is a great revision tool and has proven to be successful with both Key Stage 3 and Key Stage 4 students, particularly low prior attainers, as it teaches them different techniques to help them actively learn the vocabulary. 'Five a day MFL' works by encouraging students to revise little and often for a vocabulary test, instead of leaving it all until the last minute. This is an excellent routine for students to get into, especially since we have moved away from modular assessment and have moved towards linear assessment with the introduction of the new MFL GCSE. This idea could also be adapted for other subjects.

Students are provided with a guided vocabulary revision sheet, which includes a variety of five-minute exercises that the students should complete at home each day in the lead-up to their vocabulary test. These activities could start off simple and progressively become more challenging, with less support given each time. Students should complete the exercises from memory where possible and then use the vocabulary list to check their own answers. By breaking the learning up into bite-sized chunks, students should find revision much more manageable and less overwhelming.

The sheet could start with a simple matching-up exercise, where students link the English words or images with their target language translations. In the second exercise, students could select the correct target language spelling from three or four options.

This could be followed by several gap-fill activities, where students are given the words in the target language, each time with different letters missing that they have to fill in. Perhaps the first half of the word could be provided, with students adding the final letters, or every other letter could be given. Students could be asked to fill in the missing vowels or missing consonants, or to rewrite the letters of a scrambled word in the correct order.

For the final exercise, students will hopefully be able to translate each word in full successfully, without support. You could even provide sentences in the target language with gaps that students have to fill in with the most appropriate word, with its correct spelling.

An example worksheet (in Spanish) can be downloaded from the online resources.

MFL Trivial Pursuit®

'Fun, challenging and competitive.'

These resources are aimed at GCSE students, but can be adapted for other abilities or even other subjects!

You will need a set of counters (one counter per student), the Trivial Pursuit® board and a set of cards (one board and set per group), and one reflection sheet per student. Example cards and reflection sheets can be downloaded from the online resources. Students work in small groups of three or four. They take it in turns to move their counter around the coloured squares on the board. There are six colours, which each represent a different topic. A teammate picks up a card from the pile and reads out the word/phrase next to the colour that the player has landed on. They could read out the word in either English or the target language. The player then tries to translate the word or phrase while their teammate checks the answer. If they translate the word correctly, they can move a space; otherwise, they stay where they are and the turn passes to another member of the group.

When a student lands on a white square, they can choose the topic, and if they answer correctly they are allowed to shade in part of the circle on their sheet in the corresponding colour. The winner is the first student with all sections of their circle coloured in with the six different colours.

Throughout the game, students should make a note of any new vocabulary on their reflections sheet. At the end, give them time to complete the reflections sheet and think carefully about which topics in particular they did well on and which they found difficult – and then decide how best to develop their knowledge of this vocabulary.

Memrise

'Memrise has really helped me with vocab, Miss!'

Educational apps and websites such as Quizlet have been around for a while now. Students seem to really enjoy the competitive element and teachers are often able to easily track their progress.

Memrise (www.memrise.com) analogises vocabulary learning to growing flowers. Each vocabulary item is a seed that needs to be planted (learned), and then watered regularly (reviewed) in order for it to grow into a flower (stay in the long-term memory). It introduces two vocabulary items at a time on virtual flashcards, then tests its users on these words through a series of short games. This could be choosing the translation from one of the options or typing in the spelling of the translated word. By prompting users to 'water their plants' repeatedly, the vocabulary is more likely to stay in the long-term memory.

Memrise encourages on-the-go learning, using a smart device. There is also an offline mode, so users don't need to worry if they have no Wi-Fi access or if they run out of data. It is flexible, as it allows you to input your own vocabulary or find courses added by other users and then easily share these with your students. With its attractive and user-friendly interface, it's not surprising that Memrise is so popular with both students and teachers. Best of all, it's free to use!

There are weekly, monthly and all-time leaderboards, making it very easy to monitor students' progress and award prizes to those who are putting in the effort. This is also a great way to motivate those students who need an incentive to work a bit harder. From experience, a quick positive email home to parents always goes a long way too!

Taking it further

Set up a lunchtime or after-school Memrise club to give students more opportunities to earn extra points. This is also helpful for those who are unable to access it at home.

Highlighter splat

'Students seem to enjoy the competitive element and there is little opportunity for them to go off task.'

I'd like to give a huge thank you to Bronagh Dooris (@MissDooris) for sharing this idea. This is another low-prep activity that can be used for any topic and is great for reviewing new vocabulary that has just been introduced.

'Highlighter splat' is a quick activity that enables you to check how much vocabulary students have retained. It requires little preparation beforehand and the answers can be checked in the lesson, so no marking is necessary later on.

Firstly, introduce new vocabulary as you normally would. Students then work in pairs, with each pair being given a list of this vocabulary between them and a different-coloured highlighter each. The teacher reads the translation of the words in a random order, and students have to race to highlight the correct word on the list. The winner is the player who has highlighted the most words.

If a student highlights the wrong word, ask them to circle it so that they know that word could still be read out. This could be done from English to the target language, vice versa or even both ways.

Taking it further

With a more able group, students could be given a paragraph instead and have to race to find the vocabulary within.

Bonus idea ★

Instead of a translation exercise, this could be done as a listening exercise to check whether students can make the link between the written and spoken word.

Vocab pop

'How can I make vocabulary revision a bit more exciting?'

A fast-paced vocabulary revision exercise, which is great in the run-up to any exams.

Prepare a large grid of vocabulary, with some of the English words and some of the target language translations missing. After being introduced to and practising the new vocabulary, this is a good way to check how much your students have retained. Give each student a sheet and play a song in the target language (there is a wide range available on YouTube and Spotify). They have the duration of the song to translate as many of the words/phrases on the sheet as possible, and should do this from memory. Setting the time limit of the duration of a song keeps the pace going and increases motivation.

Next, discuss the answers as a class and allow students to mark their own work and fill in any gaps. You may wish to ask them to do their marking in a different-coloured pen so that both you and they can see where there are gaps in their knowledge. While going through the answers, ask students to discuss different ways to remember each of the words – often, the sillier these are, the better, as students are more likely to remember them.

Once they have finished marking their answers, students can add up their scores and set themselves a higher target for next time. Some students may need help with target setting to make sure that the targets are appropriately challenging but realistic. You can come back to this activity next lesson and again the week after, and enjoy seeing the look on your students' faces when they realise they have improved and met or exceeded their targets.

Teaching tip

An example worksheet in Spanish can be found in the online resources for this book.

Taking it further

Ask students to produce flashcards for homework of the words they found difficult and learn these off by heart for next lesson.

Dominoes

'This dominoes activity can be used to help students retain new vocabulary.'

There are a ton of games that can be used in the MFL classroom, and while I would not recommend using them all lesson, every lesson, they can play an important part in the teaching of MFL by keeping students motivated.

Prepare a set of domino cards before the lesson. These should include familiar language based on a topic you are currently covering. Each card should have a word in English on the left and, on the right, a different word in the target language that matches up to an English word on another card.

This game works well following the vocabulary grids activity (Idea 75). Give each student at least one card. As a challenge, provide some students with multiple cards. One student starts off the game by standing up and reading aloud the target language word on their card. The student with the matching English word stands up, says the translation and the next target language word. If successful, this should continue until you have returned to the first student who spoke. You will need to listen carefully throughout and make sure that the correct person stands up each time, as well as helping students with any tricky pronunciation.

Once you have finished, ask students to swap cards and play again. You will find that students will speed up after a few rounds, as they are finding it easier to recognise the vocabulary.

Alternatively, print off a few sets of the dominoes cards and allow groups of students to line these up in order on their tables. Award a prize to the first group to complete this.

Vocabulary grids

'This helps students to keep a record of new vocabulary and retain it.'

This idea is useful when introducing new vocabulary.

Instead of just providing students with a vocabulary sheet of the target language phrases with their English translations, this exercise requires students to actively engage with the new language.

Prepare a grid of four columns, using the headings 'Target language', 'English', 'Clue' and 'Test'. The first column should have unfamiliar words or phrases written in the target language. Print one copy per student. Before introducing the vocabulary, you could ask students to scan through the words to see whether there are any that they think they recognise or could guess. Perhaps there are some cognates. Students could also colour-code the different genders by highlighting any nouns in two different colours depending on whether they are masculine or feminine.

Next, while you are introducing the vocabulary, ask students to fill in the second column with the English translations. Students should then discuss ways to remember the vocabulary (see Idea 79) and write down any ideas they have in the third column. Throughout the lesson (and even in future lessons), as you refer back to certain words, remind students of the clues to help them remember the translations.

At the end of the lesson or at the beginning of the next lesson, students fold over or cover up the first column, then in the fourth column they translate the word in the second, using the notes in the third column to help them. This exercise could also be done from the target language into English.

Teaching tip

An example Spanish worksheet can be downloaded from the online resources for this book.

Taking it further

Ask students to keep practising these words independently until they know them all off by heart. They could tick or highlight a word when they know it.

Dictionary race

'Tengo un topo en mi cara.'

Dictionary skills are an important part of the MFL student's repertoire and I think it's necessary to train them in how to use dictionaries successfully as early as possible, in order for them to become independent. Here is another tried-and-tested activity that will give your students the opportunity to practise this skill.

Leaving the development of dictionary skills too late will make a rod for your own back, as students will be asking you for translations every other minute. Those who choose not to ask you for the translations may head to every MFL teacher's arch enemy, the dreaded Google Translate, which usually produces some interesting results. I believe that it's best to teach this skill from Key Stage 3, although I know that it can be tricky, as some students don't know how to use an English dictionary.

It is worth noting that Google Translate, when used correctly, can be an effective tool – for example when translating individual words – as it gives the definitions of the different translations, enabling the student to make an informed decision. Problems can arise when students try to type in full sentences expecting an accurate translation, as it doesn't take context into account.

Type the quote at the top of the page into Google Translate and it will tell you that I have a mole on my face. Type in the word *topo* on its own and you will see that *topo* does indeed mean 'mole', but it is a mole that you might find in your garden and not on your skin! I have seen students confuse the words *también* and *demasiado* on numerous occasions – the former meaning 'too' (as in 'also') and the latter meaning 'too' (as in 'too difficult'). It is therefore important to make students aware of homonyms like these when they are translating vocabulary.

Once you have given students a demonstration on how to use a dictionary, they can do the following activity as a way to practise what they have learnt.

Produce several lists of words to be translated and print off one copy of each list per group. Students work in small groups or pairs and are given their first short list of words to translate into the target language using a dictionary. Once they have written down their translations, they quickly get them checked by you, and if they are correct, they can be given the second sheet; if not, send them back to recheck their answers. The winning group is the first one to correctly fill in all sheets and bring them to you.

Taking it further

When students have correctly translated all the vocabulary, ask them to produce sentences using these words. These sentences could be shared with the class and translated by their peers at the end of the lesson.

Scrabble®

'What games can I use to help improve my students' spelling skills?'

This is a game that gives students a chance to develop their literacy by practising the spellings of any new vocabulary.

A Google search will bring up various images of the Scrabble® pieces and how much each letter is worth. Display this on the board or print it off and laminate copies for your students so that you can easily use them over and over again.

I've used this starter activity with both Key Stage 3 and Key Stage 4 classes, and it's a fantastic way to refresh students' memories and get them thinking back to the previous lesson.

Students aim to produce a word or sentence in the target language relating to the topic covered in the last lesson. They have to think carefully about which letters will earn them the most points, while producing an accurate sentence that makes sense. They can write this in their books or on mini whiteboards.

It is worth using a timer for this exercise to help with the pace and ensure that it doesn't go on for too long. Give a prize to the student with the most points. You could even produce your own sentence and see whether any students can beat the teacher!

Kahoot

'Are we playing Kahoot this lesson, Miss?'

This fun and engaging plenary using Kahoot will allow you to instantly see students' progress.

Kahoot is a free website that allows you to make your own quizzes, which the students can play using their own devices (smartphones, laptops and tablets can all be used). Create a quiz to revise key points that you have covered in the lesson or use one of the ready-made quizzes already available. Once your quiz has been created and launched, instructions will appear on the screen inviting students to visit kahoot.it and type in the pin number and their nickname. As soon as all of the students have joined the game, you can start the quiz. Questions will be displayed on the screen, as well as four possible answers that have colour-coded symbols next to them. The same coloured symbols will appear on the students' devices and they will be given a set amount of time to select the correct one. When creating the quiz yourself beforehand, you will be able to set a time limit for each question. Students can get more points the quicker they answer. After each question, the number of students who have chosen each option is displayed on your screen, along with the correct answer and a leaderboard of scores.

At open evenings, we usually set up a Kahoot game for the primary school pupils who visit our department during their tour of the school. We generally do vocabulary quizzes, but cultural questions could also work! We've found that it creates a real buzz in our department, and it gets the prospective students excited about what lies ahead at secondary school.

Bonus idea ★

You can now set homework on Kahoot! Create quizzes for students to complete at home. They will receive instant feedback; you won't have to mark, but will still be able to monitor their understanding by downloading the challenge results and seeing how your pupils performed on individual questions.

Magical mnemonics

'How can I help my students to remember vocabulary and tricky spellings?'

Mnemonic devices are a fantastic technique for helping students to retain vocabulary. These are different methods we can use to make something easier to memorise and they are a great way to make the vocabulary stick.

In the film *Matilda*, Miss Honey taught her pupils the memorable phrase 'Mrs D Mrs I Mrs F-F-I Mrs C Mrs U Mrs L-T-Y' as a way of remembering the spelling for *difficulty*. I'm sure many of us were taught the spelling rule 'I before E except after C' in school. My sister-in-law taught my niece, Bea, to remember the spelling of beautiful by saying 'Bea u, because you are beautiful'. 'One collar, two sleeves' reminds me that the word 'necessary' has one C and two Ss – a mnemonic that would also work for the French translation. These little tricks we use to remember certain information work really well in the MFL classroom.

My French students know that *lapin* is rabbit, as rabbits sit in your lap. My Spanish students remembered that an *abogado* is a lawyer as they imagined a lawyer eating an avocado. Encourage students to come up with their own versions and discuss these as a class and keep referring back to them. Often, the more humorous these are, the better, as students have a better chance of remembering these words. According to Smith and Conti (see Idea 64), 'the more associations created by the second language learner in learning a word, the more likely they are to remember it, because each association will have the potential to serve as a retrieval cue'.

Every year I enjoy watching my Year 7 Spanish students giggle away while I teach them the difference between *anos* and *años*, why the accent is so important and why they really don't want to say, 'tengo doce *anos*' to give their age ('anos' being the plural of 'ano', or anus!). Rebecca Wylie talks about 'memory hooks' in her blog www.ontargetteaching.blogspot.com and how she uses mimes to help her students learn new vocabulary. For example, when teaching numbers in German, she mimes drying her hands for *drei* (three) and for number four (*vier* – pronounced 'fear') she throws up her hands in fright.

Here are some examples of mnemonic devices, most of which can be used for memorising vocabulary and some of which can also be used for remembering other types of information, such as grammar rules:

Rhymes: For example, 'This and these both have Ts, that and those don't' for remembering the difference between '*esto/estos*' and '*eso/esos*' in Spanish.

Music mnemonics: Music can be a great way to help your students memorise vocabulary. There is a very catchy song on YouTube for remembering the conjugation of *aller* in French: www.youtube.com/watch?v=y47eSlLSxa0

Imagery: Visualise a Komodo dragon on top of a chest of drawers to remember the French word *commode*.

Connection mnemonics: Make a link between the new information you want your students to learn and some information they already know. Sadly, I have lost most of the German I learnt in school; however, one word that has stuck in my memory all this time is *Durchfall*. I still remember my German teacher telling us how German is a very literal language, and how *Durchfall* (literally 'through-fall') means diarrhoea. I'm hoping that I will never need to use this word when on holiday in Germany!

Bonus idea ★

If students have a text that they need to memorise, ask them to write down the first letter of each word to use as a prompt while they are learning it.

Odd one out

'How can I make vocabulary revision more challenging?'

This quick activity requires little preparation and gets the students thinking hard at the start of the lesson.

Teaching tip

An example worksheet can be downloaded from the online resources.

This is a higher-order thinking task that requires students to not only translate the vocabulary into English, but also consider the relationship between words in order to spot the odd one out. Provide students with several sets of words. I tend to do four words per set, including an odd one out in each. The sets of vocabulary could be a mixture of the following:

Verbs/nouns: Make sure that your students are aware of the different characteristics of verbs and nouns. For example, in German, all nouns are capitalised, which makes them easy to tell apart from other types of words, e.g. *Auto / Handy / kaufen / Tasche* – 'kaufen' is the odd one out, as it is the only verb. However, in other languages this will not be as straightforward.

Masculine/feminine nouns: Provide students with the tools to recognise masculine and feminine nouns. For example, in French, nouns ending in '-ment' are generally masculine, whereas '-tion' and '-ssion' nouns are typically feminine, e.g. *éducation / appartement / émission / inondation* – 'appartement' is the odd one out, as the others are feminine.

Words from particular topics: Students could distinguish between vocabulary relating to different topics, e.g. *vuelo / escribir / viajar / maleta* – 'escribir' is the odd one out, as the other three are all related to travel.

Students simply translate the vocabulary, highlight the odd one out and then say why it is different. Some students may surprise you by finding a different odd one out and thinking of links you had not even considered yourself.

Bonus idea ★

For homework, ask students to create their own odd one out sheet relating to the topic you are currently studying. They can swap with their partners next lesson and complete each other's sheets as a starter activity.

Slam dunk

'Students really enjoyed competing against their peers.'

When students are lacking motivation, sometimes simply getting them up and out of their seats can be enough to re-energise them and transform a lesson. This activity engages the students and allows you to easily check how well they have retained new or previously learned vocabulary.

This works well as a plenary at the end of the lesson and, as it requires no preparation, it's also a great activity to fall back on or to have up your sleeve if your original lesson isn't going to plan. All you need is a small basketball net and a ball.

Students work in small groups and take it in turns to translate words and phrases into English. These groups can be chosen by you or by using a random group generator tool such as Class Dojo.

Read out a familiar word or phrase in the target language. This can be one from the current topic or one learnt previously. Students work in small groups and take it in turns to translate it into English. If they answer correctly, they earn points for their group and they can nominate a member of the group to attempt to throw the ball into the net. This student has the opportunity to double the points for their team if they are able to successfully get the ball into the hoop.

If the group answer incorrectly, the question passes to another team. If the other team answer correctly, they win the points. The winning team is the one with the most points at the end of the game.

Teaching tip

There is no need to go over budget – most pound shops sell these basketball sets and they can be easily stuck up on the wall or whiteboard.

Taking it further

Include some more challenging questions for your more able students or ask students to translate from English into the target language instead.

Pick 'n' mix word games

'I use these short exercises when introducing or revising vocabulary.'

Here are several games that can be used for practising vocabulary and developing students' confidence with spelling.

Gap fill: Display phrases on the board with letters missing from each word. Students say this out loud or write it down on their mini whiteboards to practise the spellings. You may wish to provide less able students with the English translation. More able students could translate these into English themselves.

J_ _g_ _l f_tb_l c_n m_s _m_g_s. → Juego al fútbol con mis amigos.

Anagrams: Provide students with sentences containing words with jumbled-up letters. They have to write these out correctly in the right order.

ej aisv ua cmniéa vcea mse ocinpas. → Je vais au cinéma avec mes copains.

Jumbled sentences: This one is similar to 'Anagrams'; however, the words in the sentence are jumbled up instead of the letters. Students write the words in the correct order.

mes vais plage à je la avec copains → Je vais à la plage avec mes copains.

Synonyms: Students are given a list of words or phrases in the target language. They have to find another way of saying them and match these up.

delicioso	enfadado	bonito
hermoso	rico	furioso

Antonyms: Give students several words or phrases in the target language and ask them to match them up with their opposites.

delicioso	grande	feliz
pequeño	triste	asqueroso

Word halves: Students are given the first half of each word and have to complete it. To make it more accessible, you may wish to give them the second half of each word, asking them to find the correct one from a list.

vie	cans	con
tento	jo	ada

Bonus idea ★

Another variation of the gap fill idea is to give students a text with words missing and ask them to fill these in. This exercise is easily differentiated by including the first letter of the missing word or having a separate sheet with the missing words in a different order for those who are struggling to complete it without.

Vocab Jenga®

'This game works really well with my GCSE groups and keeps them motivated in the run-up to their exams; however, it could be adapted for Key Stage 3 students.'

Students compete against each other in this fun game that revises vocabulary.

Put students into small groups and give each group a pack of numbered Jenga® blocks (see Idea 4) and one pack of the Trivial Pursuit® cards (see Idea 70). Students quickly build their tower, then take it in turns to translate a word or phrase read out loud from a card by one of the other players. The person who reads out the question can also check the answer on the card.

If the player has answered correctly, they can remove a block from the tower. The number written on the block is the amount of points they receive. If the tower collapses, they don't win any points and have to rebuild the tower. The aim of the game is to gain the most points and beat their teammates.

This activity could be done on a smaller level at revision sessions or at a lunchtime language club. The teacher says a word or phrase in the target language, which the students race to translate into English (or vice versa), and if they answer correctly they can remove a Jenga® tile. The player with the most points at the end of the game is the winner.

Introducing vocabulary

'The "silly voices" technique works well at Key Stage 3.'

Here are some ideas to be used when introducing students to new vocabulary, helping to make their learning more engaging.

Hearing and saying the vocabulary: Provide students with a printed-out list of vocabulary, display it on a PowerPoint or show flashcards. Say the words using different voices (high, low, fast, slow, loud, soft) and ask students to repeat the words in the same way. Alternatively, you could display the words, then ask your students to break the words down and think about how they are pronounced.

Analysing the vocabulary: Ask your students:
- to tell you what gender it is
- to think about how many syllables/letters there are
- whether there are any silent letters
- to think of ways to remember the phrases by making links between the English and target language phrase or with vocabulary they already know, e.g. *zapatos* = shoes → *zapatería* = shoe shop.

Adapting the vocabulary: Can your students:
- change words from singular to plural?
- change the tense?
- change verbs from first to third person?
- put the phrases into a sentence and extend them by adding other details?

Checking they have retained the vocabulary: After introducing a few phrases, quiz students on them using a few different activities discussed already. These should become progressively more difficult, with less support given each time.

Teaching tip

The Learning Scientists recommend the use of retrieval practice, i.e. being tested on vocabulary learnt previously, and state that 'if you practise retrieval you're more likely to remember the information later'. See more here: www.learningscientists.org/blog/2016/6/23-1

I find that introducing new vocabulary as a phrase rather than individual words, e.g. 'je joue au foot' instead of just 'le foot', helps them to remember it.

Taking it further

Suitable activities would be gap fills, memory games, highlighter splat, mini whiteboard games, or match up the translations.

Crosswords

'Crosswords are a great way to encourage students to focus on the accuracy of their spellings.'

This exercise can be used at the start of a lesson to recap prior learning and refresh students' memories. You can also do this at the end of the lesson to enable you to see how much your students have retained throughout the lesson.

Before the lesson, you will need to prepare a crossword for your students. These can be easily produced in minutes using any of the websites below. Input the clues in English and this can be done as a translation exercise. Alternatively, add an extra challenge by writing clues in the target language, e.g. una fruta verde o roja = manzana.

https://worksheets.theteacherscorner.net

The Teacher's Corner makes it easy for you to create your own printable crosswords using a range of fonts and images.

www.wordwall.net

Wordwall allows you to create a limited number of both printable and interactive crosswords for free. The interactive quizzes are engaging and give users instant feedback.

www.languagesonline.org.uk

You can also head to Languages Online, where you will find an array of ready-made interactive crosswords for students to complete on a computer or smart device. You will simply need to provide your students with the link. Use a QR code generator site such as www.qr-code-generator.com to create a QR code that students can scan to access the website more easily.

Vocab tennis

'This is helping me to work out which topics I need to revise more thoroughly before my exams.'

Other than closing your classroom windows, no preparation is required for this active and engaging revision activity.

In this activity, students are given a topic they have covered previously (e.g. holidays) and have to work in pairs and take it in turns to throw a ball to each other. When they catch the ball, they have to say a word or a phrase from that topic in the target language before they can pass it back to the other player. Students are required to think quickly because if they hesitate for too long they will lose a life. They need to be focused and listen carefully to the other player, as if they repeat a word that has already been said they will also lose a life. If they lose all three lives, they lose the game and the other student wins. It is a good idea to set a timer of a minute for each topic, and then when the time is up, you can shout out a different topic for them to practise.

Repeat this activity at the end, allowing a couple of the victors to compete against each other in front of the class. Alternatively, they could play against you and aim to 'beat the teacher'.

This game can be made more challenging by allowing students to play in a larger group. Students throw the ball at the other players at random. There is a chance that by the time a student receives the ball again, the word they were planning on saying has already been used by another player, so they will have to think quickly on their feet to come up with an alternative.

Teaching tip

You can usually pick up multipacks of sponge balls cheaply in pound shops.

Marking, feedback and improvements

Part 8

Dice improvements

'Yeah, Miss, of course I've proofread my work!'

It's important to give students ample time to read through their work and proofread for errors. This activity helps to train students to actively check through their work for errors and then try to improve it.

In this exercise, students roll the dice and complete the actions corresponding to each number. Students, even the older ones, tend to enjoy the kinaesthesia of the rolling of the dice.

Example actions could be:
1 = Check your spellings and accents carefully. Give students access to dictionaries to support them with this; alternatively, they could look through the notes in their books.
2 = Have you included connectives?
3 = Have you included an opinion? Provide students with a list of examples of each or tell them where they could find some.
4 = Have you included a past tense?
5 = Have you included a future tense? If students are struggling with forming tenses, they could use the guides in the independent learning folders (see Idea 47). They may also find the internet and textbooks helpful.
6 = Check that you have avoided repetition where possible. Provide students with a list of synonyms, e.g. instead of 'me gusta' they could use 'me mola'.

Other suggestions: Have you included a conditional? Have you included a subjunctive? Have you included quantifiers? Have you used an idiom? Have you used the third person? Before you start the activity, make sure that students understand what each of the above means and discuss examples.

Live writes

'I find it motivating to see other students' answers. It makes me work harder, as I don't want to get left behind.'

One of my favourite activities for MFL is Kayleigh Meyrick's (@MissMeyMFL) 'Live writes'. This allows you to give instant feedback to your students' written work using Google Docs. Kayleigh talks about live writes and shares lots of other great ideas for the MFL classroom on her blog: https://missmeymfl. wordpress.com.

Set up a free Google account and then open Google Docs. In a blank word document, write a question or statement for your students to respond to. Create a grid with three columns: 'Student name', 'My response' and 'Feedback'. Click 'share' and enable students to edit the document, before emailing the link to all students in your class. In the lesson, students click the link to open the document and write their response to the question at the top of the page. As all the work is on the same document, all students are able to view each other's answers, adding an element of competition.

You can then sit at your computer and watch the responses being written, giving instant constructive feedback to individual students in the third column. This column could also be used by students to ask you questions, using Dr Gianfranco Conti's L.I.F.T. (learner initiated feedback technique) method. L.I.F.T. involves students asking you questions about things they are unsure about when producing a piece of writing. They simply write these questions in the margin for you to respond to when you mark their work.

At the end of the lesson, students can log off without needing to save the work. You can then print copies for their books and mark them.

Teaching tip

L.I.F.T. is learner initiated feedback technique. You can find more at https://gianfrancoconti. wordpress. com/2015/07/30/l-i-f-t-an-effective-writing-proficiency-and-metacognition-enhancer.

Bonus idea ★

Before the lesson, you could also write an example paragraph and display this at the top of the document, or you could come up with a model answer as a class at the start of the lesson and ask your students to think about which elements are essential for a successful piece of writing.

Whole-class feedback

'This saves me time that can be better spent planning good-quality lessons.'

This is a great way to cut down on marking time, while still providing your students with purposeful feedback that allows them to make improvements to their work.

Teaching tip

Many schools and departments will have a marking policy, so it may be worth discussing this with your head of department before you try out this idea.

Marking students' work, although a useful way to see how much progress they are making and whether they've understood what they've been taught, can be frustrating at times, especially when you have to mark the same errors and write out the same feedback 30 times in a row.

Whole-class feedback is a technique that is becoming increasingly common in schools. Sometimes, a more personal approach is of course required, but these whole-class feedback sheets work well when students are making the same mistakes repeatedly. They provide you with an overview of how well the class is performing and help you to plan future lessons.

When reading through a set of books, you simply fill in the whole-class feedback sheet with any comments and corrections that you would normally write in the student's book. You can then print out the same sheet for each student and ask them to carefully read through it, make their improvements, re-draft their work and glue the sheet into their books.

You can easily create your own version of a whole-class feedback sheet or use the ready-made template available in the online resources. I like to set out my feedback in a grid under the following headings:

Praise

This includes anything that has impressed me, e.g. excellent use of tenses by all, particularly the imperfect.

WOW phrases

I write down any examples of phrases or sentences that I particularly enjoyed reading, along with the name of the student who wrote each one, e.g. 'Si tuviera que decir... ' (If I had to say...) – Well done, Sophia! These students gain some form of reward.

Spellings and accents

Any words that are commonly misspelled are written correctly in here for students to easily correct their errors. I make sure to include translations of words that are similar, e.g. *pero/perro*, so as not to confuse the students.

Genders/adjective agreements

I make a note of any genders that students are repeatedly getting wrong, e.g. *LA televisión* (not *el*). I also remind students about adjective agreements.

Verbs/tenses

I use this box to address any misconceptions relating to verbs and tenses, e.g. *son* = they are / *hay* = there are.

Other errors

These might include missing words or incorrect use of punctuation.

I also include the date and title on the sheet, so that if for some reason the students didn't write these down in the lesson when the work was originally produced, they can quickly copy this when making their improvements.

If you do create your own version as a Word document and save it, you may find that you can just adapt this slightly for another class if they have made similar errors.

Taking it further

Provide your students with a challenge sheet that they can complete once they have made their improvements. This sheet should include questions/sentences to translate based on those areas where they are making lots of mistakes and need extra practice.

Spot the errors race

'This is a useful exercise to do after you have marked a piece of writing and made a note of any common errors made by your students.'

Students compete against each other in small groups for this marking activity. This exercise can be easily adapted for different classes and could even be used in other subjects.

Teaching tip

It may be worth giving each group of students a checklist to remind them of which errors to look out for.

Ahead of the lesson, prepare several sheets with inaccurate sentences or an inaccurate paragraph in the target language. Each sheet should include similar errors and these should be the same kind of common errors made in the students' written work. It is a good idea to include the number of errors to spot in each sentence/paragraph.

For example: J'aime joue au foot avec ma parents dans la jarden. (four errors)

You will need to print off one copy of each sheet per group.

At the start of the lesson, share with the class any common errors you found in their written work and how to correct them. Once you are confident that they have all understood where they went wrong and how to correct these errors, put your students in small groups. Provide each group with the first sheet of inaccurate sentences. They then have to race the other groups to highlight and correct all the errors. As soon as they have found all the errors on the first sheet, they should bring the sheet to you to be checked. If they have corrected the errors successfully, they can take sheet number two and do the same again. The first group to highlight and correct all errors on all sheets are the winners and could be given a prize.

Visualisers

'Using a visualiser in my classroom has revolutionised my teaching.'

A visualiser is a camera that can be used to project whatever is underneath it onto the screen. This could be a worksheet, an image, a past exam paper or a piece of student work.

One way to improve the quality of students' written work is to show them an example answer using the visualiser beforehand. You can then mark this work in front of the class, providing verbal feedback as you go and talking your class through your thought processes as you are marking. Students will find it useful to see how you mark their work, and why you give particular marks and feedback.

You could use the visualiser once students have produced their piece of writing. Find a couple of examples to display to the class. Students could peer-assess, choosing two things that the student has done well and one thing that could be improved. You can talk them through the piece of writing and what feedback you would give it, addressing any common misconceptions as you go through it. It is likely that other students will have made similar errors in their own work, so allow students some time to quickly correct those errors before handing their work in.

Visualisers are also a great resource to use when modelling best practice. Before asking students to write their own paragraph, you can come up with an answer as a class that you can model on a piece of paper underneath the visualiser. I like to predict the errors that students are likely to make in their own piece of writing, and purposely make the same mistakes when writing out the model answer – usually, they will pick up on these and we can discuss these common misconceptions as a class.

Teaching tip

Film the visualiser use and upload to YouTube or the school's VLE to allow students to refresh their memory at home.

113

Padlet

'This allows my students to demonstrate what they have learnt when working independently during a lesson in the computer room.'

Padlet is a website that allows you to create your own online notice board. Students who have been given the link can add responses to be viewed instantly by yourself and their peers.

Each time I have a new class, I book a computer room and allow students time to set up a Memrise account (see Idea 71) and play the vocabulary games. Memrise enables me to monitor the leaderboards and see how far students have progressed with the vocabulary courses throughout the lesson. However, I like to use Padlet alongside this, as it allows me to check that students can then manipulate the vocabulary they have learnt using Memrise and reuse this in other contexts.

You will need to prepare the Padlet board before the lesson by creating an account with www.padlet.com, clicking 'Make a padlet', and then typing your topic title and the question you would like your students to answer at the top of the padlet. I recommend selecting the profanity filter just in case. You should also select 'Comments', as this will allow students to peer-assess and provide feedback on their classmates' work. You can then share the link with your students and allow them time to write their answers to the question and their initials, so that you know who has written what. This allows you to quickly see how well they have retained the new vocabulary. Match each student with a 'buddy', who can write a comment beneath their answer and tell them what they have done well and suggest ways to improve their answer.

After the lesson, you may wish to print off copies for students' books.

Bonus idea ★

If you have printed copies for the students' books, they can translate these sentences back into English as a starter activity in the following lesson.

Revision

Part 9

Thinking quilts

'A challenging revision exercise.'

The 'Thinking quilts' idea was originally shared by history teacher Karen Knight (@KKNTeachLearn), but has been adapted for MFL.

First prepare your thinking quilt grid. Each box should contain an item of vocabulary in the target language and should be linked to a particular topic. These topics can be written at the bottom of the grid. The number of topics and words per topic would depend on the ability of the class. Try to include the same number of words for each topic. Example topics include:

- grammar-related, e.g. adjectives/verbs/nouns or infinitives/present tense verbs/past tense verbs
- topic/vocabulary-related, e.g. holidays/school/environment.

You can see a shortened example of a thinking quilt in Spanish below. Complete examples in French and Spanish can be downloaded from the online resources.

voy a ir	va	jugaron	van a beber
jugabais	fui	iba	tenemos
tenía	eres	vamos a jugar	juego
Present tense	**Preterite tense**	**Imperfect tense**	**Near future tense**

Print off a copy for each student. Firstly, check how many of the words in the grid the students understand by giving them a set amount of time such as the duration of a target-language song, to write the English translations. Next, allow students time to make links and identify what the words have in common. Students should decide which words go with which heading and colour-code, highlighting them in different colours until it resembles a patchwork quilt.

Emoji mindmaps

'This is always a hit with the students!'

This revision idea was adapted for MFL lessons by Kayleigh Meyrick (@MissMeyMFL) and is a great way to revise vocabulary! It is a low-prep, low-stakes activity, which is a great way to build students' confidence before their exams.

Provide students with a printed sheet of emojis representing various topics, e.g. food, nature, animals. Print this off in A3 or larger if students are working in pairs or groups. Students then spend time annotating the sheet with as much vocabulary relating to the images as they can think of. For less able students, this may be individual words, but for more advanced students this could be full sentences. By the end of the activity, they will have a visual representation of how much they know and a nice little reminder of what they're capable of.

This activity also helps both you and the students see where there are gaps in their knowledge and what they need to spend more time revising before the exams. For example, perhaps they struggled to remember the names of the colours or food items, and therefore need to recap this vocabulary.

Emoji mindmaps are also a way of gauging students' ability levels and prior knowledge at the start of the year or with a new class. Use this in the first lesson back after the summer holidays and give your students about 20 minutes to annotate the page with as many words or phrases as they can remember. Tell them this is their opportunity to really show off what they know and encourage them to use a variety of tenses, opinions, etc. where possible. It's fascinating seeing what they can come up with after a six-week break and they can add to it through the year as new topics are covered.

Teaching tip

Take a leaf out of The Ideal Teacher's book (@TheIdealTeacher) and give your students a bit of extra support, by separating the emojis into different sections depending on the topic they relate to. See more information at: http:// theidealteacher.com/ emoji-vocabulary-builder-must-use.

Revision pong

'Break up the monotony of revision.'

This revision game works well with a smaller class, but several games could be played simultaneously if you have a larger class. Use this in the run-up to exams to revise anything from vocabulary to tenses.

For this exercise, you will need a set of plastic cups and a ping-pong ball. Each cup should contain cards with questions to answer or words/sentences to translate (either into English or into the target language – you decide). Place half of the cups on one end of the table and the rest of the cups on the other end of the table. Split the class into two teams and ask them to stand at either end of the table. Students take it in turns to throw a ping-pong ball into one of the cups on the opposite side of the table. Whichever cup the ball lands in contains the card with a sentence they have to translate or a question they have to answer. It helps to have some spare cards ready so that students can still take part even if they don't manage to land their ball in a cup.

I normally award points as follows but, like most of the ideas in this book, you can adapt this to suit your classes:

- three points – goal, student answered correctly and independently
- two points – goal, student answered correctly with help from teammates
- two points – no goal, student answered correctly and independently
- one point – no goal, student answered correctly with help from teammates
- zero points – no goal, incorrect answer.

The team with the most points at the end of the game wins a prize!

Get the parents involved

'I was never any good at languages, so I can't help her.'

Most parents and carers really like to be kept in the loop about what their child is doing in school, but sadly we can't always rely on our students to pass on key information to them.

We can talk to our students about the importance of revision and independent study until we are blue in the face, but it may not make a difference if the parents are unaware that they should be revising and are therefore not encouraging and supporting them at home. Often, parents will want to support their child, but don't know how. Here are a few simple ideas to get parents involved:

- Prepare an MFL information sheet that includes key dates of upcoming exams, what topic you are currently studying, what their child should be doing to revise and how often, and how they can support their child with revision at home. This could be sent home or handed out at parents' evening.
- Take a tablet or laptop with you at parents' evening and give parents a quick demo of Memrise/Quizlet, or send a letter home with instructions.
- Provide details of any recommended MFL revision guides.
- Upload revision resources to your school's VLE and give parents instructions on how to access this.
- Make parents aware of any revision resources you have given their child, or hand these out at parents' evening.

These ideas help to create a positive parent–teacher relationship and are reminders that you all want the same thing – for their child to achieve their potential.

Bonus idea

Ask your pupils to create their own revision schedule for your subject. This should say which topics they will be looking at, how they are going to revise and when exactly. Ask them to take this home and get their parents to check it and sign it.

Revision site

'Giving students ownership of their own learning and revision is a powerful tool.'

This is a cross-curricular opportunity and a chance for your students to show off their creative skills.

Rather than setting up revision plans for students, why not get them to produce their own, developing their ICT skills at the same time? Websites such as Wix or Weebly are so straightforward to navigate that students can easily set up their own pages as a revision aid.

This idea works well with GCSE groups. At the start of the school year, allow them a lesson in the computer room to set up their website, which they can then add to throughout the year as homework. As well as giving students the opportunity to prepare their own revision materials this is also a great way for them to consolidate at home what they have learned in your lessons.

Students could set up a section per topic, as well as sections for grammar. In the grammar sections, students could:

- Add an explanation in their own words of how particular tenses are formed, as well as the endings and any irregular verbs.
- Add links to YouTube tutorials they have found useful.
- Add links to Dr Gianfranco Conti's 'The Language Gym' workouts.
- Embed Powtoon videos or PowerPoint presentations using Slideshare.

In each topic, students could:

- Include links to relevant Memrise courses.
- Include vocabulary lists.
- Add links to quizzes they have created using websites such as Quizlet or Kahoot.

Bonus idea ★

This could be made into a competition where you choose the best website and give the student a prize for their efforts.

Revision clocks

'This revision strategy works particularly well with GCSE students in the run-up to their exams.'

Geography teacher Becky Russell (@teachgeogblog) uses this clock sheet as a way to help her students revise a particular topic and to gather their ideas in one place. This idea can be easily adapted for MFL.

Each student is given a sheet that has an image of a clock in the centre, with 12 sections around it. Each of the sections will have a heading relating to a particular topic. The idea is that, in an hour-long revision session, students can spend five minutes per section brainstorming key vocabulary and structures for each of the different headings. This could be shortened to half an hour, with just two and a half minutes dedicated to each section. Students can also get creative, adding colour and images.

To make the revision session even more focused, you could include short exercises in each of the sections. Students can spend five minutes completing each exercise, instead of just brainstorming vocabulary. For example, this could be phrases to translate into English or into the target language, or a gap-fill exercise.

Teaching tip

The best revision clocks could be scanned and shared on the school's VLE for pupils to access and use to guide their independent study. Award prizes for the best ones.

Bonus idea

This revision tool could also be used as a way of structuring students' writing. Students could be asked to take the sheet home and brainstorm vocabulary for headings such as 'Key verbs' (present, past, future), 'Adjectives', 'Opinion phrases', 'Time phrases', 'Nouns', etc. They could bring this in next lesson to help them with their written work.

Revision survival kits

'It is really helpful having all of the information in one place and not having to waste time searching for it all.'

Each year, I like to give my Year 11 students a revision survival kit. Previously, I found that I was giving out lots of separate revision sheets, which would just get lost. The revision survival kit makes it easier for my students, as all of their most important resources are kept in the same place, in a booklet that they can take home.

Here are some ideas of what to include:

- Revision techniques.
- Tips for being successful in the exams.
- Important information, such as key dates of exams.
- Revision schedule for the months leading up to the exams. I add all of the topics and make sure that these are repeated and spread out.
- Links to useful revision websites/apps (exam board website, Language Gym, Memrise, Quizlet, Languages Online), as well as the QR codes, which students can scan using their smart devices for easier access. I also leave space next to each website on the sheet so that students can write down their usernames and passwords.
- Vocabulary revision worksheets.
- Examples of questions from previous exam papers.

I put each booklet in a plastic wallet and sometimes add in a few sweets to provide students with an extra bit of motivation while they are revising.

Retrieval practice challenge grids

'If you don't use it, you'll lose it.'

This is a starter activity in which students are required to retrieve from their memory information from last lesson, last week, last term and (where appropriate) last year.

Kate Jones (@87History) teaches history and came up with the retrieval practice challenge grid idea, but this can be easily used in MFL, or indeed other subjects. Kate talks about her retrieval practice challenge grids, along with other ideas, on her website: https://lovetoteach87.com. This highly effective revision strategy can be used at the start of a lesson. The idea is that regularly returning to topics covered previously and encouraging students to retrieve previously gained knowledge is more conducive to learning than covering it once and not seeing it again until they revise for their exams.

Prior to the lesson, you will need to create a PowerPoint slide showing a grid of four columns and four rows. The top row could contain the following headings: 'Last lesson (1 point)', 'Last week (2 points)', 'Last term (3 points)' and 'Last year (4 points)'. The other boxes should be filled with sentences to translate (or even questions to answer) relating to topics that your students have covered previously. Give students about five minutes to translate as many of the phrases as possible into English. I like to print off a blank grid for students to write their answers in and then glue into their exercise books. Go through the answers with your class, allowing them to peer-assess and add up their points. The further back the topic is, the more points they earn.

Teaching tip

This activity can be further differentiated by including translations aimed at a range of abilities. I like to include a bronze, silver and gold question for each of the columns.